A Publication in the Berrett-Koehler Organizational Performance Series

Richard A. Swanson &
Barbara L. Swanson
Series Editors

Other books in this series include

Analysis for Improving Performance
Corporate Creativity
Effective Training Strategies
Human Resource Development Research Handbook
Structured On-the-Job Training

Results

HOW TO ASSESS PERFORMANCE, LEARNING, AND PERCEPTIONS IN ORGANIZATIONS

RICHARD A. SWANSON

ELWOOD F. HOLTON III

Berrett-Koehler Publishers, Inc.
San Francisco

Berrett-Koehler Publishers, Inc.
450 Sansome Street, Suite 1200
San Francisco, CA 94111-3320
Tel: (415) 288-0260   Fax: (415) 362-2512
www.bkpub.com

ORDERING INFORMATION

Individual sales. Berrett-Koehler publications are available through most bookstores. They can also be ordered direct from Berrett-Koehler at the address above.

Quantity sales. Special discounts are available on quantity purchases by corporations, associations, and others. For details, contact the "Special Sales Department" at the Berrett-Koehler address above.

Orders for college textbook/course adoption use. Please contact Berrett-Koehler Publishers at the address above.

Orders by U.S. trade bookstores and wholesalers. Please contact Publishers Group West, 1700 Fourth Street, Berkeley, CA 94710. Tel: 510-528-1444; Fax: 510-528-3444.

Printed in the United States of America

 Printed on acid-free and recycled paper that is composed of 50% recycled fiber, including 10% postconsumer waste.

Library of Congress Cataloging-in-Publication Data

Swanson, Richard A., 1942-
    Results : how to assess performance, learning, and perceptions in organizations / Richard A. Swanson, Elwood F. Holton III.
    p. cm. — (A publication in the Berrett-Koehler organizational performance series)
    Includes bibliographical references and index.
    ISBN 1-57675-044-2 (alk. paper)
    1. Employees—Rating of. 2. Performance standards. I. Holton, Ed, 1957-. II. Title. III. Series.
    HF5549.5.R3 S815 1999
    658.3'125—dc21
                               99-17437
                                CIP

First Edition

03 02 01 00 99   10 9 8 7 6 5 4 3 2 1

Book Production: Pleasant Run Publishing Services
Composition: Classic Typography
Cartoons created by Eric Robert Rosenberger

To
Barbara L. Swanson
and
Karen S. Holton

Contents

▼

CONTENTS

Preface

▼

Writing a book is a lengthy journey. And like most other long journeys, this one had some unexpected events along the way. Our original motivation for writing this book was to try to do something significant about improving the state of evaluation practice in human resource development (HRD). That desire has only increased as a result of writing this book, and our hopes are high.

During our writing journey, we regularly had to face oncoming blinding lights—the reminders to us that despite decades of preaching, cajoling, and encouraging, the HRD profession still typically does not assess the results of HRD interventions (in general or specifically, within organization development or personnel training and development). The purpose of this book is to improve this condition.

The HRD process has five phases: analyze, propose, create, implement, and assess. As a systematic process, the five phases connect and build on each other. Even so, there is a special connection between the beginning and end of the process—the analysis and assessment phases. These are the two phases that directly connect to the primary mission and goal of the organization. The analysis phase defines the performance improvement opportunity in the host organization, the intervention, and the expected results (see Swanson, 1996). The assessment phase focuses on the actual results of the intervention, which is what this book is all about.

Most HRD practitioners do not find the currently available evaluation and assessment resources compelling, friendly, complete, or usable. Thus, our challenge was to present a usable system for results assessment. We have created a system that is friendly, usable, accessible, and consistent with current research and theory. This book sets out the integrated Results Assessment System with a concise five-step process, a straightforward planning mechanism, and practical measurement tools. We, and a number of our practitioner colleagues, have used the Results Assessment System successfully in numerous organizations.

ACKNOWLEDGMENTS

Fortunately we did not have to travel on this writing and learning journey alone. Two authors are not always better than one, but in our case the coauthoring process has welded a professional partnership and personal friendship unlike anything else we have experienced. We can only hope that it lasts years to come. Our publisher and editor, Steve Piersanti, is a man of integrity beyond any of his peers. It is a privilege to work with him and Berrett-Koehler Publishers. At times other people—practitioners and scholars—gave us a needed push. Reid A. Bates, James M. Brown, Manuel A. Carvalho, Mertis A. Edwards, Deane B. Gradous, Sara Jane Hope, Brent W. Mattson, Carol P. McCoy, Timothy R. McClernon, Sharon S. Naquin, Lawrence J. Quartana, Lilanthi Ravishankar, Dian L. Seyler, Gary R. Sisson, Catherine M. Sleezer, Barbara L. Swanson, and Richard J. Torraco contributed to our ideas, thinking, and the clarity of our presentation. We thank them also.

Richard A. Swanson
St. Paul, Minnesota, USA
Elwood F. Holton III
Baton Rouge, Louisiana, USA

PART 1

Assessing Results

1

An Assessment System That Works

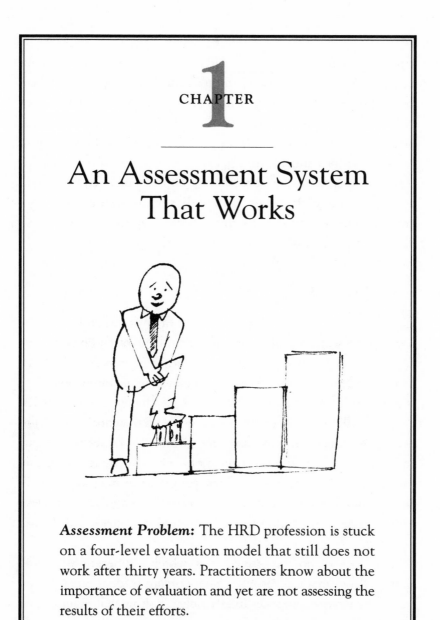

Assessment Problem: The HRD profession is stuck on a four-level evaluation model that still does not work after thirty years. Practitioners know about the importance of evaluation and yet are not assessing the results of their efforts.

▼

Human resource development (HRD) professionals achieve results in organizations by developing or unleashing expertise in individuals for the purpose of improving performance at the organizational, work process, work group, and individual levels. This book will show you how to assess those results. More specifically, it will show you how to assess performance, learning, and perception results from HRD interventions and other development efforts sponsored by leaders, managers, and work groups. Many other professions are also concerned about performance, learning, and perception results and will find this practical book useful in their work.

This Is Not an Evaluation Book

Go to any bookshelf of management or organizational books, and look up the word *evaluation* in the index. How often do you think the word is mentioned? We cannot find it. Yet members of the HRD profession consistently talk about evaluation while rarely practicing it in the field. What is going on here? One clue is in the terms you do find in the indexes of most business books—words like *performance, assessment,* and *measurement.* Evaluation professionals tend to be consultants who study educational and government programs rather than build core organizational performance and processes. We have come to realize that the word *evaluation* evokes a negative schoolhouse picture and the idea of assigning grades on ill-defined activities.

This book is about *assessing results,* which is different from evaluation. Assessment of results is a core organizational process. Surveys of evaluation practices in HRD clearly show that practitioners view evaluation as optional (Bassi and Cheney, 1996). The well-known four-level evaluation model (Kirkpatrick, 1998) has failed the profession for a number of reasons (Alliger and Janak, 1989; Bassi and Cheney, 1996; Dixon, 1990; Holton, 1996; Newstrom,

1995; Swanson, 1998), but a key failure is its emphasis on reactions versus the fundamental performance results of the host organization.

Readers will feel initial comfort with our Results Assessment System relative to the four-level evaluation model because at first glance they are not radically different from one another. A second glance, however, reveals fundamental and substantial differences in their assessment and evaluation priorities and the completeness of the practical research-based tools offered in the Results Assessment System.

HRD has not been a serious performance partner in most organizations, and thirty years of the four-level evaluation model has done little to change this condition. This leaves top managers and clients typically asking for nothing more than participant reactions evaluations—"smile sheets"—that do not correlate with either learning or performance. When top managers finally decide to do a serious assessment, it is usually in response to a crisis or to their own judgment that things have gone awry. Invariably it comes too late.

THE REWARDS OF RESULTS

Why assess and report results? Imagine for a moment an organization that does not measure its financial results. How would its members know if the organization were successful? Or suppose the organization does not measure its manufacturing productivity. How would it stay competitive? What if it did not assess its product ability to meet customers' needs? Its products could become obsolete without the organization's realizing it. Suppose it did not assess its efficiency in using resources. It would quickly cease to be cost-effective. In short, it is doubtful that such an organization would survive. HRD is no different.

This book presents a guide for building world-class human resource development that is successful, competitive, meets customers' needs, and is cost-effective. The Results Assessment System presented in this book is a practical and credible system for assessing results from development efforts. It can be applied to any HRD program in any organization.

ACCOUNTABILITY IN PRACTICE

If HRD is to be a core organizational process, it must act like one and hold itself accountable for obtaining results through its interventions. The corporate school and human relations models of development practice that exist simply because they are "good for employees" is outdated. HRD practitioners unwilling to accept demands for accountability are being downsized and outsourced. The good news is that HRD that can deliver results is more highly valued today in organizations than at any other time in recent history. The challenging news for many practitioners is that moving from optional nice-to-do to core process activities brings with it accountability for results. Almost everything that is important in organizations is assessed. Failure to assess something is to say to the organization and its employees that it is not important. Assessment informs people that what is being assessed is important to the organization's success.

Consider your own professional practice. What do you make your top priority and pay the most attention to? What aspects of employee activity do you think are most important to the organization? How do you know they are important, and thus a high priority for you? The odds are good that someone measures and monitors these things. More than likely, what is assessed is somebody else's perception of the results you achieve.

By not assessing results, HRD tells the organization that it does not view itself as important. By reporting only participant reactions to or perceptions of a development activity, the status of HRD is not much higher. Even if the organization truly views HRD as important, it cannot put HRD on par with other core organizational processes without more substantive assessment of results. Thus, results assessment is essential to establishing HRD as a core organizational process.

We believe that the biggest barriers to results assessment in HRD are fear of accountability and the inadequate evaluation models and methods that permeate the profession. Many practitioners are afraid to find out whether their interventions really make a difference. By not asking the questions, they do not have to come to grips with their fear that results really are not occurring. A typical workplace scenario consists of the busy HRD practitioner doing what the company wants, feeling successful, and not being regularly required to prove the added value that results from HRD contributions. With a full agenda of important development and delivery tasks, the busy professional finds it difficult to measure results.

This is a false security. Almost all important organizational processes and functions are regularly assessed in terms of their effectiveness, efficiency, and bottom-line contributions to the enterprise. Fortunately, outstanding results can regularly be obtained when sound HRD practices are used. In addition, it has been clearly established that effectiveness data, particularly bottom-line performance results, are the key to gaining support for the HRD function from top management (Kusy, 1988). It is clearly irrational *not* to assess and report results.

THE SATISFACTION OF ASSESSING RESULTS

Those who assess results find that it eventually becomes a source of tremendous pride and satisfaction. A shift to results assessment causes change. In the short term it may even cause you to be embarrassed a little when you discover that an organization development intervention does not work or to cancel the further offering of a training program. Maybe you will have to think differently about your practice and learn some new skills.

But it is worth it. There is no greater source of professional satis-faction in HRD than having an executive, manager, or group of employees ask for your help to improve their effectiveness and then seeing actual results. And assessing the results provides data to demonstrate it to everyone in the organization.

The ultimate gain is for HRD to become a core organizational process and a performance partner to executives, managers, and employees because the HRD professionals know what really gets results. Assessing and reporting results is the key, and the Results Assessment System covered in this book really works.

KEY POINTS TO REMEMBER

▼

- Even after thirty years, the four-level evaluation model has proved ineffective.
- Assessment and evaluation are different. *Assessment* of results is a core organizational process. *Evaluation* is optional.
- Assessing and reporting results is an essential element of all core organizational functions and processes.
- The Results Assessment System sets the priorities of performance, learning, and perception outcomes.

CHAPTER 2

Core Concepts of the Results Assessment System

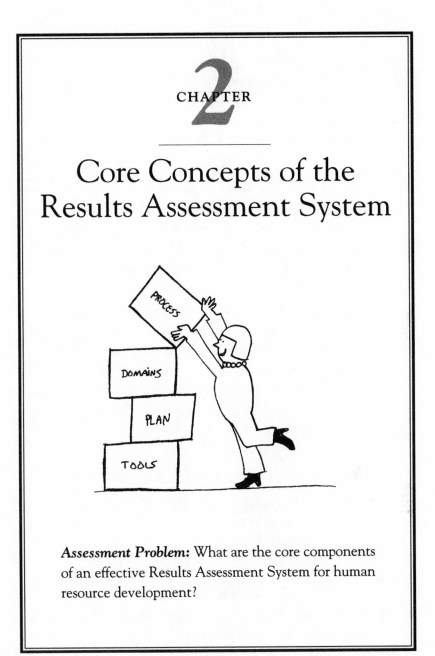

Assessment Problem: What are the core components of an effective Results Assessment System for human resource development?

▼

One of the greatest strengths of the Results Assessment System is that it is an integrated system firmly grounded in HRD theory and research. This chapter provides an overview of the system and frames it in the larger HRD development and improvement process. These core concepts are the foundation of the rest of this book.

HUMAN RESOURCE DEVELOPMENT PROCESS

The process of change and improvement within organizations, work processes, and individuals is fairly universal. Although each specialization may have its own vocabulary and variations, the core process does not change much. Human resource development can be characterized as having five phases (Table 2.1). Almost all models of HRD or organizational performance change contain a final phase in which outcomes are assessed. Unfortunately, the final phase is the one most often ignored. This book focuses on the final phase.

It is critical to recognize that HRD professionals work their HRD process in the context of a host organization. This is illustrated in our worldview model of HRD in Figure 2.1. Study this systems model, and you will see the following.

Table 2.1. The Human Resource Development Process

Phase	Description
1. **Analyze**	Determine performance requirements and their relationship to HRD interventions.
2. **Propose**	Design strategies and propose appropriate interventions.
3. **Create**	Create intervention components (such as design, logistics, program, materials).
4. **Implement**	Implement the intervention (organization development and personnel training and development).
5. **Assess**	Determine if desired results have been achieved.

- The five-phase HRD process parallels other organizational processes.
- HRD's primary goal is to assist the host organization in producing outputs more effectively.
- The mission and goals of the host organization interact with HRD (and its mission and goals).
- The host organization inputs connect to HRD (as well as to other processes in the organization).
- The host organization operates in a larger environment of political, economic, and cultural forces that envelop and penetrate the organization, its processes, HRD, and the results.

This systems worldview model has value for clarifying the important role of results assessment in HRD. HRD is a means to achieve some larger result in an organization. It is for this reason that results assessment is not optional, for it is the results that affect the organization and ultimately provide outputs that customers desire. For HRD to be a core organizational process, its results must be assessed. This model also has utility in keeping the big issues surrounding results assessment in perspective in that the world does not begin and end with HRD.

Familiar models of improvement, change, and development are variations of this core development model. For example, Lewin's organization development model (unfreeze, move, and refreeze) is an elementary view of the journey of change with assessment driving the process. It is fun to think of this and related HRD processes from both the individual perspective and the total organizational perspective of moving from an existing place to a new place. Almost all of the HRD models are variations of the core five-phase HRD process shown in Table 2.1 and call for assessment of results—for example:

Figure 2.1. Systems World-View Model of Human Resource Development

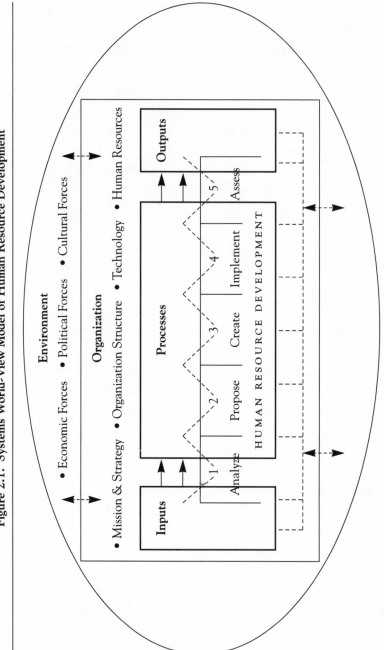

- General model of planned change (entering and contracting, diagnosing, planning and implementing change, and evaluation and institutionalizing change)
- Quality improvement PDCP (plan-do-check-act cycle) cycle
- ADDIE (analysis, design, develop, implement, and evaluate) training process
- Action learning sequence (data collection, reflection, synthesis, options, agreement, presentation, and implementation)

THE RESULTS ASSESSMENT SYSTEM

Results assessment, which reflects the last phase of the five-phase HRD process, can be defined as determining if desired outputs have been achieved by the HRD interventions. The Results Assessment System presented in this book has four basic components: a process, results domains, a plan, and tools (Table 2.2). The process describes the general steps necessary to conduct a results assessment in an organization. Domains define the possible range of results that can be assessed. The plan identifies all the key decisions that must be made to design a results assessment. And the tools provide the means to measure results. The tools are covered in Part Two of the book (Chapters Six through Ten) and expanded on for special situations in Part Three (Chapters Eleven through Fourteen).

Table 2.2. Components of the Results Assessment System

Component	Key Question
Process	What are the general steps necessary to conduct a results assessment in an organization?
Domains	What domains of outcomes should be assessed within HRD?
Plan	What are the key decisions that must be made to design a results assessment, including outcome domains to assess?
Tools	How are results measured?

RESULTS ASSESSMENT PROCESS

The basic process of the Results Assessment System is illustrated in Figure 2.2. This five-step process for assessing results provides a simple and direct journey from analysis inputs to decision outputs.

Several aspects of this process are worth noting here:

- To be most effective, results assessment requires strong front-end analysis. It is hard to assess outcomes if the goals are not well defined.
- This process has an action orientation in that the final outcome is presumed to be decisions about HRD interventions and actions taken to maintain, change, or eliminate programs. The purpose is not research.
- The five steps present a simple and logical progression of activities essential to effective results assessment.
- Considerable emphasis is placed on defining expected results and properly interpreting them, in addition to the issues of developing good measures.
- These five steps describe the steps to take within an organization to put these tools to work.

RESULTS DOMAINS

In this book you will learn how to measure results within three domains: performance, learning, and perception, each of which has two options within it.

Performance Results

The options in the performance results domain are system and financial:

System: The units of mission-related outputs in the form of goods and/or services having value to the customer and that are related to the core organizational, work processes, and group or individual contributors in the organization

Core Concepts of the Results Assessment System

Figure 2.2. Results Assessment Process

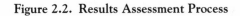

Front-End Analysis Inputs

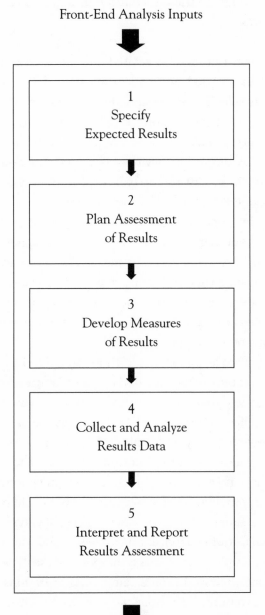

Decision Outputs

Financial: The conversion of the output units of goods and/or services attributable to the intervention into money and financial
interpretation

The assessment of mission-related outputs looks at the bottom
line—things like 50,000 cars made, the patient lived, or 5,000 service contracts sold. Those pursuing improvements in an organization face a key dilemma: mission-related outputs. Although the focal
point is the output goal, the means, or *driver,* of that goal may look
very different. A simple analogy would be a sporting event in which
the goal is to win by getting the ball through the hoop more times
than the opponent and thereby scoring points.

Scoring points, and enough to beat the opponent, is the mission-
related output, but there are a wide variety of development actions—
performance drivers—that could be pursued by the coach, assistant
coaches, the team owner, the offensive players or strategy, the defen-
sive players or strategy, and individual players. Connecting the performance drivers to the system outputs of performance is critical to
understanding performance results.

The best time to figure out this relationship is during the front-end
analysis phase. It is there that you discover, for example, that the coach
has no strategy and that the club president has no sound plan for hir-
ing and firing players based on the performance requirements of the
team. Without this front-end analysis, decision makers in complex
organizations will often implement simplistic or invalid performance
drivers that have no real connection to the system performance goals.

Other than providing useful metaphors, what could performance
analogies from simple games like basketball possibly have to do with
complex manufacturing, service, governmental, and educational organizations? Yet simplistic analogies from sports can sadly be the extent
of the up-front analysis. In some complex organizations this is it in
terms of the extent of their thoughts prior to committing to performance drivers. *The Witch Doctors: Making Sense of the Management
Gurus* (Micklewait and Woolridge, 1996) is an extended analysis of

the false promises made by well-meaning people about their "special brews" (performance drivers) without any substantial evidence of their connection to the system outputs (performance outcomes). More detailed attention will be given to the issues of performance drivers and performance outcomes in Chapters Six and Fourteen.

Learning Results

The options in the learning results domain are knowledge and expertise:

Knowledge: Mental achievement acquired through study and experience

Expertise: Human behaviors having effective results and optimal efficiency, acquired through study and experience within a specialized domain

Knowledge, an intellectual or cognitive result of learning experiences, is the basic learning result. It is lodged in a person's mind. Measures of knowledge confirm the level of knowledge held by individuals within a particular subject area. In terms of being both effective and efficient, paper-and-pencil tests are the primary means of measuring knowledge.

Human expertise is the second category of learning—the more complex learning result category. People with expertise have knowledge and are able to act on that knowledge. The effective and efficient ability to act on knowledge generally comes from experience beyond core knowledge. Measuring human expertise requires that an individual demonstrate his or her behavior in a real setting or a simulated setting. When assessing learning results, we generally recommend that both knowledge results and expertise results be measured. And it is logical that knowledge can be measured some time before expertise in that the learner needs time to gain experience. The span of time will vary depending on the complexity of the area of expertise being developed.

Perception Results

This options in the perception results domain are participant perceptions and stakeholder perceptions:

Participant perceptions: Perceptions of people with firsthand experience with systems, processes, goods, and/or services
Stakeholder perceptions: Perceptions of leaders of systems and/or
people with a vested interest in the desired results and the
means of achieving them

Of the three domains, the perceptions domain has the lowest cost
and lowest return. It is lowest in terms of cost in the sense that simple, short, and standardized perceptions rating forms can be produced
for participants and stakeholders. It is lowest in terms of return because
it provides the least valid information about performance outcomes.

Perception results are perceptual states held by human beings that
you are concerned about. Measures of perceptions systematically
access this information from selected groups of people. The mantra
for the perception results domain should be: (1) get the data, (2) do
not spend a disproportionate amount of resources to get them, and
(3) do not overinterpret the data. We recommend that you get these
data only as long as they are not used as a substitute for measuring
performance results or learning results. For example, self-reports by
people that they have learned something is not a measure of what
they learned. We also recommend that you get perceptions results
data from both the participants and the stakeholders. Thus, from a
general planning perspective, commit to both participant and stakeholder perception results in the Results Assessment Plan.

TIME TO GET MOVING

To deal effectively with this range of content may seem impossible
for such a small book. Our approach is to be selective in our presen-

tation, not exhaustive. True to the title of the book, we want you to be able to get your own results in terms of assessing performance, learning, and perception results. We also want you to be able to begin obtaining valid and reliable results data quickly.

There is nothing like getting results to motivate individuals and organizations to make a commitment. If you are able to measure and present positive results—"the consequence of a particular action, operation, or course" (*American Heritage*, 1993, p. 1164)—you increase the odds of obtaining and then continuing support from everyone at every level. If the results are not positive, you want to be the first to know so as to alter your course of action. Professionals who turn their backs on assessing results are likely to miss an important piece of the joy that comes from seeing improvements in people, organizations, and society. The job is clear: to get on with the task of adopting a sound assessment process and to put it to work.

KEY POINTS TO REMEMBER

▼

- The five phases of the HRD process are analyze, propose, create, implement, and assess.
- The assessment of results is about outcomes—the consequence of a particular action, operation, or course.
- The components of the Results Assessment System are process, domains, plan, and tools.
- The domains of the Results Assessment System are performance (system and financial), learning (knowledge and expertise), and perceptions (participant and stakeholder).
- There is nothing like getting results to motivate individuals and organizations to make a commitment.

3

Sales Communication Case Study

Assessment Problem: At a general level, what does a results assessment look like, and how does the process actually work?

▼

The application of the Results Assessment System in this case study concerns a sales communication improvement effort for sales personnel in a major insurance company. These individuals sell insurance plans to other companies for their employees. The performance improvement intervention in this case involves 167 sales personnel and their 24 sales managers across the nation over a six-month period. The results of this effort proved to be positive on a number of fronts; astonishingly, the $2,352,300 financial gain attributed to the program had an eight-to-one (800 percent) return on investment in less than a year.

For years, this insurance company had supported a goal-setting process for sales and general communication skills training for their sales personnel, even though there was no real evidence that it was producing business results. The overriding logic was that salespeople need general communications knowledge and sales managers need to establish goals in order to get sales performance results. Finally, without any evidence of actual performance outcomes (or even documented evidence of resulting communication knowledge and expertise), the goal-setting plus training-program approach came under fire as to whether it was worth the expense.

It is important to note that a new vice president of performance consulting and training had walked into a department whose staff had committed themselves to the assessment of participant reactions as the core of their evaluation efforts. His staff members were pursuing these under a false assumption: that participant reactions are a proxy for learning (not true), that learning is a proxy for behavior (not true), and that behavior is a proxy for performance (not true). Because the staff had been unable to figure out a more substantive way to assess their results, they settled for participant reactions, thinking that the reactions in fact were highly correlated with the other levels. The new vice president was aware of the research that clearly demonstrates there is no correlation between participant reactions ("happy sheets") and learning, let alone later behavior and performance (see Alliger and Janak, 1989; Alliger, Tannenbaum, Bennett, Traver, and Shotland, 1997; Dixon, 1990; Holton, 1996; Swanson and Fentress, 1975).

Because the new vice president of performance consulting and training had knowledge of measurement, was aware of the importance of up-front performance analysis, and had a limited base of support for the old effort, he began by conducting a performance analysis around the sales process. The diagnosis confirmed an initial perception that the company was losing business as a result of inadequate transactional communications skills among the sales personnel and their clients. The analysis included observation of actual sales transactions and follow-up interviews with former clients that revealed fundamental communication deficiencies. The analysis also revealed that the sales managers did not provide adequate support or attention to the sales process and sales personnel. The performance consulting staff then analyzed and documented a precise profile of the communication expertise required to succeed in the closing of sales transactions (see Swanson, 1996, for a detailed look at the analysis method used for both of these phases).

This profile of communication expertise and system support became the basis of a sales communication project that included (1) a new sales communication training program and (2) a new performance appraisal system used for sales personnel back on the job. Sales managers, as well as sales personnel, received training. Sales managers were trained in coaching and appraising the new communication skills. They were also recruited to assist in the role-playing assessments of the expertise of sales personnel during training and in conducting the follow-up coaching and performance appraisals back on the job.

The insurance company already had a system for tracking sales by individuals, office, region, and product line. Thus, the core system outcome of sales was already tracked as a regular part of the business.

In most organizations, outputs that have value to the customer, sometimes referred to as mission-related outputs (Holton, 1998) or as outputs of the spine of the system (Swanson, 1996), are systematically measured. We call these performance results *system outcomes*. This company also calculated the average financial worth of a sale (gross and net), which allows system outcomes to be converted into *financial outcomes*. (In fact, most organizations can do this. Usually somebody has these numbers.) The immediate stakeholders in the insurance company did not initially know the financial measures around sales. They became clear through the application of the Results Assessment System.

This sales communication case study will be referred to throughout the book to illustrate the Results Assessment System. There are three other major topics for the case study:

- Plan for assessing the results: What was the specific plan for applying the Results Assessment System to the sales communication case?
- Tools for measuring the results: What were the measurement tools and measurement process considerations for assessing performance, learning, and perception results?
- Reporting the results: What results data and conclusions are drawn from the sales communication improvement effort?

PLAN FOR ASSESSING THE RESULTS

The detailed planning decisions are recorded on the Results Assessment Plan, a one-page planning document central to the entire assessment process. This plan bounds the total results assessment effort. It is presented in detail in Chapter Four. All measurement questions and the general strategies for answering them are contained within this planning document. The Results Assessment Plan has five parts and asks five fundamental questions:

1. Expected results: Of the six options of result outcomes, what choices will be pursued for this assessment effort? (We focus on this question in this chapter.)
2. Data collection time line: Within each of the results options selected, where along the time line of events will data be collected?
3. Data comparisons: Will the data collected along the time line be compared to data outside that time line?
4. Data analysis plan: What is the analysis plan for comparing data for each option selected?
5. Execution details: What planning and execution points should be heeded in executing the plan?

The first planning step, the *expected results*, requires a basic decision if all six, or some subset of the six result options, will be pursued for this assessment. For this case, the question is, "Which of the six options will be pursued in assessing the sales communication case?"

The planning discussion in this chapter will focus on this first planning step of dealing with the three results domains of performance, learning, and perceptions. And, for simplicity, the three results domains will be discussed in reverse order of importance: perceptions, learning, and then performance.

Expected Perception Results

This step in the plan for measuring results in the realm of perception is relatively easy. Remember what they are:

Participant perceptions: Perceptions of people with firsthand experience with the services and/or goods produced or the means of producing the results

Stakeholder perceptions: Perceptions of leaders of those organizations and/or people with a vested interest in the desired results and the means of achieving them

In the case of sales communication improvement, the primary focus of the intervention was on the insurance sales personnel as the participants and the primary stakeholders were the sales managers. The plan was to assess the perceptions of both.

Expected Learning Results

Learning in the Results Assessment System has two core categories of results: knowledge and expertise. Recall their definitions:

Knowledge: Mental achievement acquired through study and experience
Expertise: Human behaviors, having effective results and optimal efficiency, acquired through study and experience within a specialized domain

In the sales communication case, the knowledge of the sales communication aspect of the sales process was organized into ten content units that matched the flow of expert work behavior. Thus, within the core sales communication tasks, the knowledge elements and the elements of demonstrating expertise used the same content structure. In another instance the knowledge structure could more closely follow a theory model, while the expertise structure could follow a practice structure. Although the two categories of learning in this case adhere to the same general structure, one is about knowing and the other is about doing. Both were deemed important to assess.

Expected Performance Results

Performance in the Results Assessment System has two core categories of results, system and financial results. Remember their definitions:

System: The units of mission-related outputs in the form of goods
and/or services having value to the customer and outputs that
are related to the core organizational, work processes, group,
and individual contributors in the organization

Financial: Converting the worth of the units of outputs of goods
and/or services into money

In the sales communication case, the performance driver focused
on the sales communication process, the role of the manager, the
reward system, and the communication expertise of the sales personnel. The performance outcome was an actual sale. Remember that
the vice president of performance consulting inherited a weak performance driver in the form of a training program in general communication skills. There was no substantial evidence that the training
program improved on the performance outcome of sales. Through
analysis of the sales situation and the execution of a comprehensive
performance improvement effort (not just training), there was confidence that there was a connection between the new performance
drivers—the sales communication improvement efforts—and the performance goal of improved sales. Thus, the performance goal of
increased sales was used as the measure of system results.

The number of sales—the system results—had no financial meaning in this case. In terms of measuring financial results for the sales
communication case, the conversion of the system's units of performance—sales—times the financial worth of each sale became a
multiplication problem. One way to express these financial results
is to take the net profit from all the increased sales and subtract the
cost of the sales communication improvement program. Simple
financial analyses such as these show if the financial return exceeded
the financial benefit and the financial return on investment.

Thus, in planning the sales communication performance results
assessment, there was a commitment to measuring both system

results (performance outcomes) and financial results. In a different situation, the performance results at the system option might have to move from a system performance outcome to a system performance driver—for example, regular adherence to the sales process, including its managerial oversight, the consistent execution of the reward system, and the honoring on the communication interaction principles in the actual work setting. Remember that the premise here is that these elements were determined to be critical components of an effective sales process. It is almost impossible to convert system performance driver results data directly into financial results. Given enough time, performance drivers should show themselves in terms of performance outcomes. In the interim, there must be an intermediate financial valuing of the driver results. One way is to have responsible leaders estimate the value of the performance driver. This is like saying, "What would you pay to have this factor exist in your organization?" This important idea of financially valuing system drivers in the short term is discussed in greater detail in Chapter Seven.

In summary, the expected results for the sales communication improvement case—step 1 of the Results Assessment Plan—is to carry out all six results options: performance results (system and financial), learning results (knowledge and expertise), and satisfaction results (participant and stakeholder).

TOOLS FOR MEASURING THE RESULTS

Six measurement tools were used in the sales communication case; brief overviews of them follow described for the result categories.

Performance Results

Both system results and financial results were measured. System results were measured in terms of the performance outcomes of actual sales. The good news in this case is that the company already had a sales tracking system that was very good. It recorded each sale and attributed it to an individual salesperson, office, and region. This information was collected and reported daily through the management information system.

The company also already tracked and reported financial results. Because the compensation of sales personnel was tied to sales performance, the worth of each sale was known and reported. Again, the company recorded each sale and attributed it to an individual salesperson, office, and region. This information was collected and reported daily through the management information system.

Learning Results

Both knowledge results and expertise results were measured. For knowledge, a paper-and-pencil test of forty multiple-choice items was used. It measured the participant's knowledge of the ten content areas of sales communication, with four items per content area.

In terms of expertise, a ten-part rating form was developed for sales managers trained as expert raters to observe and rate sales personnel on the dimensions of sales communication expertise. This was done during a simulation at the end of training and back on the job.

Perception Results

Both participant results and stakeholder perceptions were measured. Standard perception forms of one page or less from the Results Assessment System were used for assessing the perceptions of participants and stakeholders.

REPORTING THE RESULTS

The results report is an executive summary of the effectiveness of a program. The intention is that every program offering be assessed in terms of its results and that the results be reported to the appropriate stakeholders in the organization. Results reports have a standard format, standard sections, and a standard way of reporting data. The reports are short—generally two to five pages in length.

There are standard sections to the results report:

Results Report Overview (Contents of Page 1)
- Organization and Program Identification Heading
- Program Purpose
- Program Description
- Results Summary
- Approval
- Distribution List

Assessment Results (Contents of Page 2 to the end)
- Performance Results
- Learning Results
- Perceptions Results
- Improvement Proposal

Because the results report is an executive summary, there are almost always more assessment data available than are contained in the report. The department retains these additional data and uses them for tracking and improving specific elements of the program and for responding to specific evaluation inquiries. The full results report for the communication improvement case study is presented in Chapter Ten. Here are the highlights of it.

Performance Results
System. In total, 24 sales from the 167 participating sales personnel were reported and verified as having been a direct result of the sales communication improvement effort during the six

months following the training portion of the program. These business results were fully attributed to the program. No comparison group was needed or used.

Financial. The net profit from the reported sales attributable to the sales communication effort was $2,352,300. The cost of the program was $288,000. The conservative estimate of the financial return on investment in the six months was eight to one. The standard Results Assessment System financial goal is two to one. Thus, the sales communication improvement training attained 400 percent of the original goal.

Learning Results

Knowledge. A score of 30 on the forty-item knowledge test was established as the minimum knowledge standard for sales personnel. At the end of training, the average knowledge score was 34.5 (115 percent of goal).

Expertise. Using a ten-part structured rating form, expert raters measured the expertise of participants on the dimensions of sales communication expertise. An average rating of 2.0 on the 1–3 scale was determined to meet the client's expectations of expertise. At the end of training it was 2.129 (106 percent of goal), and sixty days after training it was 2.33 (117 percent of goal).

Perception Results

Participants. The average participant satisfaction rating by 167 sales personnel was 3.72 on a scale of 1–4. The results goal was 2.5. The sales communication training portion component of the effort attained 149 percent of the goal of getting a 2.5 or higher average rating on the satisfaction scale.

Stakeholders. The average satisfaction rating by sales managers sixty days after the program was 3.68 compared to the goal of

2.5. The stakeholder satisfaction results achieved 147 percent of the goal of a rating of 2.5 or higher on the satisfaction scale.

CONCLUSION

In this case study the Results Assessment System was successfully applied to the sales communication effort, and the data provided convincing evidence of the effectiveness of the intervention.

Although the case study validates the workability of the Results Assessment System, several related events took place. The senior vice president of the company read the final assessment report and spoke to the vice president of performance consulting twice about the findings and methodology. The impressive results and the formal reporting caused her to pass the report on to the company president. This led to another tier of exchanges, including a workshop on the Results Assessment System for eighteen other professionals in the company. Simultaneously, a pocket of resistance arose from two other development teams in the company from their perception of being pressured into implementing the system.

The critical element in this case was the front-end performance analysis and the commitment to improve the results of the corporation through purposeful and systematic follow-through. The training-alone alternative that had been used in the past had never yielded results beyond participant satisfaction with the training event. Going from vantage point of performance to participant satisfaction is relatively easy; going from participant satisfaction vantage point to system performance is almost impossible. Thus, this case started with performance analysis, went down to learning and system change issues, and ended in performance improvement. The secondary issues of participant and sponsor satisfaction results were viewed as a bonus, and the knowledge and expertise results were critical in achieving the performance results.

KEY POINTS TO REMEMBER

▼

- Prior to this case, the communication aspect of sales had been thought of as elusive or "soft" in that it was not clear how communication expertise directly affected results.
- The new sales communication performance improvement effort, through HRD, was based on a thorough up-front analysis and systematic execution. These features moved the effort from "soft" to "hard" in terms of gaining results in all three results domains.
- The Results Assessment System was able to evaluate and document the extremely positive results from the sales communication effort. Upper management enthusiastically received the findings.

CHAPTER

4

Planning Results Assessments

Assessment Problem: How do I plan a results assessment? More specifically, given the complexity of the situation and the wide range of alternatives, how do I construct a sound and workable plan that will guide the entire results assessment process?

▼

The Results Assessment System provides a comprehensive yet easy-to-use template that guides the entire assessment. The worksheet used in the system is a simple and important tool for making and working the plan.

RESULTS ASSESSMENT PLANNING

Each of the assessment planning decisions is recorded on the Results Assessment Plan worksheet shown in Figure 4.1. Completing this planning sheet leads you through the five core decisions you need to make about each results option in the Results Assessment System. Later chapters discuss each decision in detail and provide sufficient information for you to make sound decisions about each of these questions. These core decisions are in response to the following questions:

1. In terms of results, which of the three domains and six options will be measured?
2. When will the results data be collected (before, during, and/or after the intervention)?
3. How will the data be analyzed?
4. What measurement tools and details are needed to execute the assessment plan?
5. Will the results be compared to another cycle, a standard, or a norm?

The rows (A-F) of the worksheet represent the three results domains and the six results options presented in Chapter Two. You will recall that all six results options were checked for the sales communication case. The columns on the worksheet, numbered 1-5, represent the five core decisions the planner makes in relation to each of the results domains and options.

Decision 1: *Which of the three results domains and six results options will be measured?* Chapter Two took you through the process of deciding which of the three domains (performance, learning, and

Figure 4.1. Sample Results Assessment Plan Worksheet

Program Title: _____
Prepared by: _____ Date _____
Approved by: _____

1 Expected Results (Choose from 3 results and 2 options for each)	2 Data Collection Time Line (Select data collection points pertaining to the program or intervention)	3 Compare (Use option 7-Cycle, 8-Standard, or 9-Norm if pre-post assessments are not used)	4 Data Analysis Plan (Specify data to be compared to answer the assessment of each domain row A–F; e.g. D3 ↔ D11)	5 Execution Details (Highlight measures, timing, implementation, etc.)
Performance Results	Before 1 2 During 3 4 After 5 6	7 8 9		
A. System				
B. Financial check				
Learning Results	Before 1 2 During 3 4 After 5 6	7 8 9		
C. Knowledge				
D. Expertise check				
Perception Results	Before 1 2 During 3 4 After 5 6	7 8 9		
E. Participants				
F. Stakeholders check				

perceptions) and two options within each domain you will choose to measure. Your choices should be checked in the "Expected Results" column (column 1).

It is not always appropriate or necessary to choose all three domains or all options. For example, when we were consulting with two separate divisions in a large corporation that were located in two states, it was as if we were working with two different organizations. In one division HRD had established itself as a major contributor, and we could almost automatically think of all six results options (A-F) as being appropriate: system performance, financial performance, knowledge outcomes, expertise outcomes, participant perceptions, and stakeholder perceptions. Anything fewer than all six generally was based on practical limitations, such as time limitations or high redundancy between two options.

In contrast, the HRD department in the other division had never established itself as a major business process. For example, it never engaged in fundamental performance analysis (the discovery of performance requirements and solutions). Worse yet, it did not even have a track record of assessing learning results from any of its programs. As a result, the idea of promising performance results was administratively outside the reach of the HRD work group. Its first challenge was to gain credibility through assessing and reporting the knowledge and expertise results (options C and D) from its programs and then grow into performance.

Decision 2: *When will results data be collected (before, during, and/or after the intervention)?* Data pertaining to the program or intervention will be collected within a data collection time line and recorded in column 2 of the worksheet. Each option selected can potentially be measured before, during, and after the intervention. For example, it may be possible to assess system performance outcomes before, during, and after an intervention. In addition, it may be desirable to measure a results option several times before, during, and after the intervention so as to get an average score or to plot a trend. This choice is represented on the worksheet by two intervals of time in the before stage (time line boxes 1 and 2), two in the during stage (time line boxes 3 and 4), and two in the after stage (time line boxes 5 and 6).

A common example might be giving a knowledge test before the beginning of a training program to see how much participants already know (Knowledge time line box 2) and then again at the end of the program (Knowledge time line box 4). Another example might be taking expertise measures thirty days (Expertise time line box 5) and ninety days (Expertise time line box 6) after training.

Decision 3: *Will the results be compared to another cycle, a standard, or a norm?* All results measures need to be compared to something to judge the quality of outcomes achieved. However, it is not always appropriate or desirable to make within-group comparisons (for example, a person's expertise at one time compared to that same person's expertise at another time). Many times it is desirable to compare results to some external measure. Other comparison options are shown in boxes 7, 8, and 9 in column 3.

Box 7 refers to another cycle of the same program (e.g., the May group in Executive Development compared to the August group in Executive Development). This could also be a control group that did not participate in the program.

Box 8 refers to a standard: an attainment level that has previously verified meaning—for example, having a 90 percent or higher on-time arrival of flights, a sales standard of $4 million per month for the sales region, or an average participant satisfaction rating that is positive. These standards should not be arbitrary. They should be referenced to existing data and information. For example, research demonstrates clearly that gaining new knowledge and expertise can be hard work, not necessarily an easy or fun experience. Thus, the standard is to have an acceptable average rating of 2.5 or higher (positive) on a 4.0 scale. In this instance, the results goal is the pursuit of high learning results without negative participant feelings, not the pursuit of the highest possible participant reaction.

Box 9 is a norm. A norm comes from a large database that provides averages used as a point of comparison—for example, industry averages or benchmarks. At some point, norms, if they are confirmed, can work their way into being standards.

Decision 4: *How will the data be analyzed?* Just what data will be collected, compared, and presented as part of the final evaluation report for a specific intervention? The data analysis plan allows planners to state what data will be compared to what to assess the results for each of the six results options selected.

An example here is participant perceptions at the end of a program noted on the plan with an "X" in the Participant row, column 4 (Participant-4) compared to a standard of 2.5 or higher on a 1-4 scale noted on the plan in Participant row, column 8 (Participant-8). The data analysis plan is a comparison of the two: Participant-4 ↔ Participant-8. Here are two other examples:

- Average expertise before attending the program compared to expertise after participating in the program (Expertise-2 ↔ Expertise-4)
- Financial return on investment of staff-managed performance improvement efforts compared to external consultant-managed efforts (Financial-6 ↔ Financial-7)

Decision 5: *What other information is needed to execute the assessment plan?* The fifth column records details about two critical areas of results assessment: measures to be used and implementation details. Measures used, discussed in detail in Part Two of this book, include the full range of possibilities—for example, production data, market share data, paper-and-pencil tests, supervisor performance ratings, customer surveys, and cost data. Implementation details might include any specifics about the actual measurement steps and their timing—for example, how the measures will be collected, the instruments distributed and collected, and the timing of the data collection. The general timing on the data collection time line will need to be made more specific, such as the day before the intervention, the last hour of the intervention, or sixty days following the intervention.

COMMUNICATION CASE STUDY
RESULTS ASSESSMENT PLAN

Figure 4.2 is a sample completed Results Assessment Plan for the sales communication case study.

System Results

The decision was to measure actual sales attributed to individual salespeople and to do this up to sixty days following the training portion of the improvement effort (System-6). The comparison was made against the average sales of the same group over the sixty days prior to the intervention (System-1). Thus, total sales gains or losses by individuals and/or group before and after the intervention are recorded (System-6 ↔ System-1).

Financial Results

Since there was a decision to assess system results (row A) in the form of actual sales (performance outcomes, not performance drivers), they could easily convert these sales into financial numbers in this case. The total number of changes in sales (Financial-6 minus Financial-1) was multiplied by the net worth of an average sale (Financial-9). (The direct cost of the program could also be factored in; this is discussed in Chapter Seven.) And the final numbers are to be compared to the very conservative Results Assessment System two-to-one standard for return on investment (Financial-6-ROI ↔ Financial-8-ROI).

Knowledge

The plan calls for the assessment of knowledge results for the purpose of confirming the presence of core knowledge required of the sales communication theory and practice expected of salespeople. A

Figure 4.2. Sample Completed Results Assessment Plan Worksheet

Program Title: **Sales Communication**
Prepared by: _____ Date _____
Approved by: _____

	1 Expected Results (Choose from 3 results and 2 options for each)	**2** Data Collection Time Line (Select data collection points pertaining to the program or intervention)	**3** Compare (Use option 7-Cycle, 8-Standard, or 9-Norm if pre-post assessments are not used)	**4** Data Analysis Plan (Specify data to be compared to answer the assessment of each domain row A–F; e.g. D3 ↔ D11)	**5** Execution Details (Highlight measures, timing, implementation, etc.)
	check	Before 1 2 — During 3 4 — After 5 6	7 8 9		
Performance Results					
A. System	✓	1 ✓; 6 ✓		A6 ↔ A1	sales attributed to sales intervention
B. Financial	✓	2 ✓; 6 ✓	8 ✓	B6 ROI ↔ B8 ROI	attributed sales × $net/sale
Learning Results					
C. Knowledge	✓	1 ✓; 4 ✓	7 ✓	C4 ↔ C8	40-item knowledge test
D. Expertise	✓	2 ✓; 4 ✓; 5 ✓	7 ✓	D2 ↔ D4 & D5	10-dimension/3-point scale
Perception Results					
E. Participants	✓	1 ✓; 4 ✓	7 ✓	E4 ↔ E8	std. instrument/goal = 2.5
F. Stakeholders	✓		8 ✓	E6 ↔ E8	std. instrument/60 days after/goal = 2.5

forty-item multiple-choice test of the ten content areas of effective sales communication will be administered at the end of the training segment (Knowledge-4) and will be compared to the minimum standard score of 30 correct (Knowledge-8) that was established through the pilot test of the training program (Knowledge-4 ↔ Knowledge-8).

Expertise

A simple rating instrument of the ten communication factors was to be used before, during, and after the communication development intervention. Sales managers serve as trained observers to rate the participants in a role-playing situation using a ten-category instrument, with each category rated as exceeds standards (3 points), meets standards (2 points), and below standards (1 point). The goal was for all participants to reach or exceed an average expertise score of 2.0-Expertise-4 on the time line. Also to be reported are the before (Expertise-2) and after (Expertise-5) scores of expertise. The Expertise-2, Expertise-4, and Expertise-5 average scores were to be compared to the 2.0 standard, Expertise-8.

Participant Perceptions

The standardized participant rating form from the Results Assessment System was filled out by each participant at the completion of the training component of the improvement effort (Participant-4). These ratings were averaged and compared to the established standard of 2.5 or higher on a 1-4 scale (Participant-8). Thus, the comparison was: Participant-4 ↔ Participant-8.

Stakeholder Perceptions

Each supervisor of each participant filled out the standardized stakeholder perception rating form from the Results Assessment System sixty days following the intervention (Stakeholder-6). The plan was to collect supervisor perception ratings, average them, and compare them to the established positive standard of 2.5 or higher on a 1-4 scale (Stakeholder-8). It made no sense to assess supervisor perceptions prior to this point because they would not have had a chance to observe any results from improvement effort. Thus, the comparison was: Stakeholder-6 ↔ Stakeholder-8.

CONCLUSION

The Results Assessment Plan, one of the four major components of the Results Assessment System, provides clarity to the assessment process, keeps the assessment process under control, and provides assessment process continuity from HRD intervention to HRD intervention.

KEY POINTS TO REMEMBER

▼

- The Results Assessment Plan reduces planning decisions to five key questions.
- The outcome of the planning process is a concise summary of measurement steps to be executed and documentation to archive for future use or audit.
- A practical assessment plan makes the results assessment much easier.
- A completed plan serves as an invaluable communication tool to keep all parties informed about the results assessment process.

5

Practical and Credible Assessment of Results

Assessment Problem: How do I maximize the likeli-hood that results assessment will be practical enough to be implemented and credible with users?

▼

When you hear the word *measurement*, what do you think of? Research? Statistics? Time-consuming work? Confusion? In fact, results assessments and measurement tools that work are none of these things. In this chapter, we look at some basic principles that will help you build a Results Assessment Plan that is useful to your organization because it is practical and has credibility with users. Practical systems are economical enough to get implemented and do not impose a bigger burden on users than is justified by the benefits they provide. Credible systems are viewed by decision makers as providing information they can rely on for decisions and by users as leading to correct decisions.

PLANNING PRACTICAL ASSESSMENT SYSTEMS

Planning an assessment can be expensive and result in a product that is difficult to use and ultimately not used. There are so many rival ideas about evaluation and measurement that it can very quickly become confusing. In fact, the primary reason for the six-option results menu of the Results Assessment System is to reduce the overwhelming number of options that experts in measurement and evaluation can put before us. This framing of the options to six makes assessment work manageable from the beginning.

Many professional evaluators forget that the job of measurement and assessment is not evaluation but something more fundamental: producing results. Having too many options partially explains why many newcomers to measurement say that "it costs too much" or "it takes too much time" and why they usually select simple schemes that are attractive but ultimately inadequate. This chapter covers basic principles that will help you build a measurement system that is practical enough to last.

Deciding Which Interventions to Measure

It may surprise you that it is not worth the effort to assess the results of all interventions. Many seminars and books would have you believe that you should assess the results of every single intervention that you sponsor, surely an intimidating prospect. Assessing results takes resources—time, energy, and money. Although this book shows you how to do it economically, it still makes sense to devote your resources to assessing only results that count.

Assessment resources should be devoted to those programs with high potential to benefit from assessment. The key is knowing how to prioritize among the interventions. Consider these results quality criteria:

- Is the intervention being conducted for the purpose of improving performance?
  If not, it probably means people do not care about results.
- Is the intervention forecasted to have significant and meaningful results?
  If not, do not waste your measurement resources.
- Are the costs of not getting results high enough to justify the effort?
  If not, then sponsors may not care about your data.
- Are the people who care about the results important organizational partners?
  If not, then what do you gain?
- If the intervention is shown not to produce results, would it be eliminated or changed?
  If not, then results must not really matter or there is some other reason the assessment has to be done.
- Are the results really in question?
  If you are sure it works, maybe you can postpone measuring results until you have looked at more questionable programs.

If you can't answer yes to all the above questions, then consider devoting your assessment resources to other interventions.

A purist would also ask why you are conducting the intervention in the first place. A more pragmatic perspective is that you are likely reading this book with a whole stable full of programs of varying quality and importance. Programs with less impact stay alive in organizations for many reasons, including legal requirements, tradition, management "pets," or simply because people like them. Do not use any of these as an excuse to waste resources on meaningless interventions. Unless you have unlimited assessment resources, you have to prioritize.

Deciding Where to Start

Looking at results assessment processes through a strictly technical lens would suggest that every important intervention's results should be completely assessed, using all the domains in the Results Assessment System. The hard reality is that not every organization is ready to do everything at once. An organization that has never assessed any interventions may be lucky to implement knowledge assessment, while another one that has conducted regular testing is ready to move ahead to performance assessment.

The most important thing is to start, and it is okay to start wherever it is comfortable. When results assessment is viewed through an organizational change lens, you may not get people to change too much too fast. Start with what is practical and achievable. Typically once some results are assessed, users will start to ask questions about other results measures and will push to do more once the value of this work is clear.

It is not okay to settle for a low level of results assessment. If results are important, then measurement systems should continue to improve until they address most of the measurement domains in this book and are providing the information for sound decisions. So, start where comfortable, and then improve.

Using Existing Measurement Systems

It is always amazing to see the faces of HRD professionals when they realize how much results assessment information they need is already available in other organizational measurement systems. Typically HRD professionals begin an intervention assuming that everything they need will have to be created from scratch. The truth is exactly the opposite, particularly in the performance domain.

If the intervention is targeted at real performance-related needs that are important, the chances are good that someone in the organization is already measuring the necessary information. Do not reinvent systems. The closer that assessment systems are to established organizational measurement systems, the more likely it is that they will last.

Considering Accuracy

The purpose of results assessment is to enable the organization to make sound decisions about interventions. The level of accuracy needed for organizational decisions is considerably less than that needed for research. Your task is to find the "sweet spot" on the accuracy continuum so that you are buying enough accuracy to exceed management expectations slightly so you earn maximum credibility. If you buy more accuracy than that, you are wasting resources.

Consider an organization development program that is likely to return the typical financial return of 800 percent in a year or less (Swanson, 1998). Will it really matter to management if your measure is off by 50 percentage points, that is, you report 750 percent or 800 percent? Will you make any better decision about the program if you knew for sure the return was 800 percent? If the answer is yes, then pay for that degree of accuracy. If the answer is no, accept less. Often, giving up a modest amount of accuracy will save considerable resources.

Statisticians call this a *confidence interval*. In practical terms this means to consider how wide a range of accuracy you are willing to accept. The wider the range is, the more economical the measurement is.

Fast-Cycle Measurement Processes

Fast-cycle measurement is an iterative process that works in situations where interventions are repeated with some frequency. The idea is simple but powerful. The first time you assess results, do so with a very wide confidence interval. That is, do not buy much accuracy. If the results are overwhelmingly good, then stop.

If the initial measurement suggests a range of return from 500 to 1,000 percent, that may be close enough. If step 1 pinpoints a possible problem or is not convincing, invest more to assess with greater accuracy to get a more accurate measurement. For example, if the initial assessment suggests a return of 100 to 500 percent, we are not convinced. We need to know more because we may accept 500 percent but not 100 percent.

Many programs will never need measurement past the first step. Resources saved there can be devoted to more accurate measurement on others. This approach works particularly well in organizations that move too fast for complete assessment processes.

Practical Sampling

There is usually little reason to assess results every time an intervention is repeated. Researchers have long known that sampling is an effective approach to reducing measurement costs with minimal loss of accuracy (that is, when it is done correctly). The basic principle of sampling is that unless conditions are substantially different, a measurement made on one group is a reasonable estimate of results for another group. So, for example, one class of managers in a company is likely to be similar to another class if it is an open enrollment class. In that case, assessing results from one class may be enough.

There are many ways to sample, including periodic cycles (for example, every other month offered), a subset of classes (for example, one of every three classes offered this month), or a subset of attendees (for example, one of every four people involved).

The best samples are usually random because they are less biased. *Random* simply means that whatever unit is used to sample (course offerings, course sections, attendees) is chosen at random. However, this is often hard to accomplish, so *purposive* samples are common in results assessment. It is up to the assessor to be sure a sample is not biased. Be sure that the people assessed are approximately representative. Remember that when final statistics are reported, they will be used to make general statements, so make sure your sample is not likely to yield unusual or unrepresentative results.

BUILDING CREDIBLE ASSESSMENT SYSTEMS

Many times, results assessments that are practical turn out not to be credible (and vice versa). The challenge is to plan an assessment that is both practical and credible. This section discusses key principles to build credibility.

Promising Only What You Can Deliver

The only thing worse than not delivering results is promising and then not delivering. Too often assessment system designers create expectations among users that cannot be fulfilled. Consider these examples:

- Promising to "prove" results when you can really only deliver "measures" of results, some of which may be less than perfect
- Promising to show that a program is the cause of performance improvement when other events may be contributing and cannot be measured separately
- Promising to deliver results more quickly than you can

- Management's promising users that results assessment will be used to make changes, when management has reserved the right not to use the results

In practice no results assessment is perfect, but perfect analyses are rarely expected in organizational decision making. Credibility builds when the limitations of a results assessment are openly acknowledged, along with its strengths. An old cliché advises us to "underpromise and overdeliver"—good advice for results assessments.

Objectivity

There can be little doubt that results assessments can be biased and can be made to lie. It should be obvious that results assessment cannot be viewed as credible if it is not conducted objectively. The credibility clearly depends on the objectivity and ethics of the assessor. Our concern here is not with those who deliberately attempt to rig results assessments, but with a widespread reluctance among HRD professionals to take an honest look at the results of their interventions. It is always puzzling to hear HRD professionals express fear of results. Why is it that they are afraid to apply to their own practice the same principles of continuous improvement that many of them teach?

The most effective professionals are those who sincerely want to know exactly how well, or poorly, their interventions are doing. These professionals constantly aim to take a hard, objective look at results because they care about their contribution to their organizations. Sometimes it hurts when interventions do not succeed, and sometimes we do not understand why they fail. At other times results assessments lead to grand celebrations for great successes. Most important, results assessments may be the most vital source of learning for HRD professionals. But high-quality learning will not occur without honest, objective results assessments.

Results Versus Formative Measures

Evaluation professionals may evaluate inputs, processes, or outputs. For example, evaluators conduct formative evaluations during program pilot tests to assess the effectiveness of a revised work process. Although this is valuable, the point is that evaluation models allow evaluators to skip measuring results. In fact, a popular evaluation scheme clearly gives permission to practitioners not to measure results (Kirkpatrick, 1998).

To the organizations in which development is embedded, it is results that are paramount. All of the learning process and in-process perception measures are important, but they are important to organizations only if they are combined with results measures. The Results Assessment System does not incorporate more formative measures because they are well handled elsewhere, not because they are not valued. It is the results component that is missing or overlooked.

Assessing Important Results, Not Just Interesting Ones

Consider this scenario. You have convinced your colleagues to conduct a results assessment. You are all clustered around a conference table, filling out the Results Assessment Plan. Excitedly, the group begins to understand that they really can execute an assessment, and they begin to say, "It would be *interesting* to know if . . ." These words will cost you more in credibility than you can imagine.

The problem is that many of the interesting things to know will never be acted on. Your credibility with managers and employees will always suffer if you collect data and then do not use them. When assessment occurs, employees generally expect the organization to act on the issues raised by the data. If nothing happens, they assume that the organization does not care, or they begin to wonder what ulterior motives are at work. Either way the organization loses. Use this decision rule to select what to measure: If a measure is not reasonably likely to be used to change subsequent interventions, discard it. Such measures may be interesting but will not lead to decisions.

CONSISTENCY AND ACCURACY: PRACTICAL CONCERNS

Measures have to possess two key characteristics to be of value: they must be *accurate* and *consistent*. Measurement experts call these two concepts, respectively, *validity* and *reliability*. Measures are said to be accurate if they measure what they are supposed to measure. For example, self-reported measures of performance on the job tend not to be very accurate because people tend to overrate themselves. A consistent measure is one that yields the same results every time it is used. A measure can be very consistent but not valid (it can measure inaccurately or measure the wrong thing). For example, a person may be quite consistent in his or her performance rating but not very accurate.

Measures used to assess results have to be both accurate and consistent. Consider the electric meter on your home. We suspect that it is very important to you that it is accurate in measuring exactly the amount of electricity you use. We also suspect that you want it to be accurate every month, not just some of the time. If it was inconsistent because it was right some months and measured too high other months, we suspect you would not be very happy. It is no different with performance measures.

Measurement experts talk about three common types of accuracy (or validity). The minimum requirement is that the content of your measure matches the content of what you are trying to measure; this is known as *content validity*. For example, for a performance rating instrument, the items on the instrument must minimally match what is required to do the job. This is usually established by subject matter experts and is done logically, not statistically.

A higher level accuracy check is to ask whether the measure really predicts the dependent variable it is supposed to predict; this is *criterion validity*. Thus, we would expect our performance rating instrument to be able to predict, or distinguish, high performers from low performers. If we find that high performers in an organization have widely varying scores on the performance rating instrument, then the instrument would not have good criterion validity. An instrument could have accurate content (appear to have the right content) but not be a good predictor, probably because important things were left off the instrument.

A third type of accuracy, known as *construct validity*, is particularly important when measuring attitudes, such as job commitment or motivation. Because they cannot be directly observed or measured like scrap or sales, we have to measure behaviors that are believed to represent the attitudes. Because indirect measures have to be used, a concern is to establish that what they actually measure is the thing they believe they are measuring. Comparing the measure to similar or related measures usually does this. For example, a motivation instrument might include a measure of whether a person arrives at work on time. In fact, this might have little to do with motivation, but rather reflect difficulties with child care or traffic problems. Care must be taken with attitude measures to be sure that they really measure the attitude you want them to.

RESULTS ASSESSMENT CHECKLIST

Use the checklist shown in Figure 5.1 to review your Results Assessment Plan and verify that it is practical and credible.

Figure 5.1. Results Assessment Checklist

Practicality

❏ Intervention chosen for assessment meets all the results quality criteria listed earlier in this chapter.

❏ Level of difficulty is achievable given the organization's prior experience with assessment.

❏ New measures created do not duplicate existing measurement systems, and all existing measures have been examined.

❏ Level of accuracy does not exceed management expectations needlessly.

❏ Level of rigor is appropriate at this stage of problem definition.

❏ Sampling is utilized if possible.

Credibility

❏ Commitments represented by the Results Assessment Plan can be met.

❏ Meaningful results other than just satisfaciton measures are being assessed.

❏ Measures selected will be accurate.

❏ Measures selected will yield consistent measures each time they are used.

KEY POINTS TO REMEMBER

▼

- Results assessment must be practical enough to be implemented and credible enough to be used to make decisions.
- Practical results assessments focus resources on assessments that can make a difference and provide just enough information to make competent decisions.
- Credible assessments are consistently perceived to offer accurate information on results that are important to the organization.

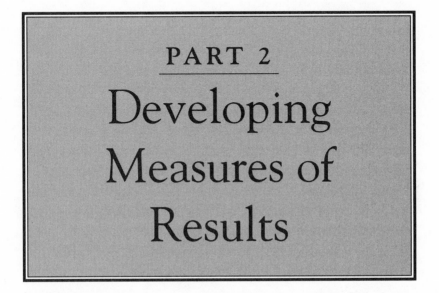

PART 2

Developing Measures of Results

CHAPTER

6

Performance Results
Measuring System Outcomes

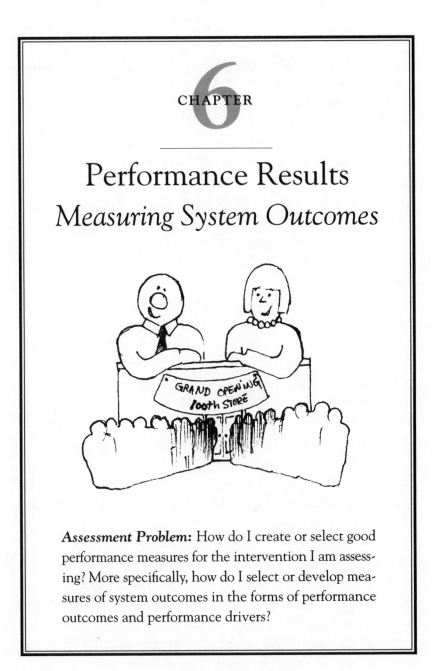

Assessment Problem: How do I create or select good performance measures for the intervention I am assessing? More specifically, how do I select or develop measures of system outcomes in the forms of performance outcomes and performance drivers?

DEVELOPING MEASURES OF RESULTS

▼

The first option within the Results Assessment System performance domain is system results, defined as the units of mission-related outputs in the form of goods or services having value to the customer or client. These goods or services are also related to the core work processes and group and individual contributors in the organization.

A fundamental realization for HRD professionals committed to improving performance is that most organizations already have methods in place to measure mission-related system outcomes. Ironically, what looks at first to be the most difficult measurement problem, measuring whole system outcomes, turns out to be much easier because existing measures can be used. To ignore performance outcomes is foolish.

The form of an intervention most likely looks different or disconnected from the outcomes. For example, organizations do not develop team behavior in a work group for the performance outcome of establishing a team. They do it so that a team can produce outputs more effectively or efficiently than a nonteam. Measuring the attainment of team characteristics can be viewed as a measure of a driver of performance, not the performance outcome itself. For professionals doing the work of developing human resources and improving work processes, this means that they must connect their efforts to the organization's mission-related goals and the expected performance outcomes. Thus, an intervention is a means to an end, not an end in itself.

Decision makers rationally try to measure "the important things," and you would presume that mission-related system outcomes are at the top of any decision maker's list. Thus, most organizations decide on what to count (the right stuff), count them in a meaningful way (accurate data), and then act on the data.

Our sales communication case is a perfect example. It is relatively easy in the sense that a sale is a sale is a sale. Sales have meaning to individual salespeople, the sales unit, and the total organization. Each sale touches the mission, the customer, and it almost always has a meaningful financial worth attached to it. The company already had an effective sales measurement system. The challenge was to understand it and use it for HRD's advantage. In assessing the system outcomes of the sales communication case, the decision was to measure the actual sales performance for each salesperson and to do this sixty days following the training portion of the improvement effort. In this work setting, sales personnel make a relatively small number of sales per year that are individually worth a great deal. Time needs to lapse in order to determine the effect, if any, that the communication program had on the sales system outcome. Sixty days were determined to be appropriate.

HOW TO THINK ABOUT MISSION-RELATED OUTPUTS

Here is an example of the thinking necessary to specify or clarify system results in the form of mission-related outputs. Publishing House sells books to customers. Publishing House has Print Shop print its books. The author writes books that Publishing House publishes and Print Shop prints. Each of these three elements—publisher, printer, and author—constitutes a larger professional book system, yet each element has its own system and subsystems. (For the sake of example, we will not include any additional systems.) And depending on the level of analysis, these three elements are viewed as systems or subsystems. At times, the three systems touch and overlap. The important lesson for professionals wanting to develop measures of performance is to isolate the system to be assessed and then identify its unit(s) of output. We call this *framing the system*.

The focus of this example is Publishing House, and the question is, "What is the output of the mission-related output of its system?" A completed transaction—a sold book—is the most likely unit of performance output. While the authors and printers have a high interest in books being sold, Print Shop will most likely see printed books (printed, bound, boxed, and shipped) as its mission-related output. If the author wrote the book for a flat fee, she would likely see the final approved manuscript as the performance output.

Again, for Publishing House, books purchased by customers are the core output—the output that has value to the customer and to Publishing House. Publishing House tracks this mission-related performance output, sales data, on an ongoing basis and also creates formal reports of books sold on a monthly basis.

Imagine that Publishing House wants to improve sales. The firm has many options it could pursue. One way is for Publishing House to improve its existing system or the processes (subsystems) in it. Another would be to expand or reshape the system. In this vein, one proposal was to improve sales in Canada by signing an exclusive agreement with Canada Books to sell Publishing House books in Canada. The direct cost of this addition to the existing Publishing House system is negligible, but it does preclude Publishing House from selling books in Canada. If it does, it reduces its profit per book sold in Canada because Canada Books takes its agreed-on percentage of each Canadian sale.

Canada Books anticipates that 15,000 copies of Publishing House books can be sold in Canada the first year. Let us say Publishing House makes $5 profit per book and agrees to give Canada Books $2 for each book sold in Canada. Here is a set of hypothetical numbers that illustrates an increase of $20,000 profit (from $25,000 to $45,000) for Publishing House obtained from a no-cost sales improvement decision. The new Canadian partner gets $30,000, from which it must pay its own costs of operation:

	Year 2000 Canadian Sales (Before "Canada Books")	Year 2001 Canadian Sales (After "Canada Books")
Total books sold	5,000	15,000
Publishing House profit	$25,000	$45,000
Canada Books income		$30,000

The major point of this example is that assessing performance results requires that mission-related performance outcomes be carefully specified. In this illustration, it was book sales. While we provide a picture of the financial implications here, you will learn more in Chapter Seven about turning system outcomes (such as book sales) into financial outcomes. Information about the mission of the system is required to begin focusing on measuring performance outcomes. The first step is to identify and frame the system being considered. In our book example, is it the publishing system, the printing system, the authoring system, or the international distribution system? The answer is that it is the publishing system: Publishing House.

Sometimes the mission-related outputs of the system are already formally documented by the people managing the system. You will need to get this documentation. Other times the system frame and its outputs exist in the minds of those who manage or direct the system, and your job is to have them confirmed by these people. In some instances, people who manage or direct the system do not have a clear definition of agreed-on units of mission-related outputs. If that is the case, you need to help these managers identify their core product or service.

PERFORMANCE OUTCOMES IN THE FORMS OF GOODS OR SERVICES

To help some more in thinking about performance outcomes and the unit of output, here are familiar categories and examples:

Goods Produced
Durable goods (hard goods), for example, cars, computers, ice skates, and highway signs
Nondurable goods (soft goods), for example, cereal, newspapers, shirts, and printed tax forms

Services Produced

Organizational services, for example, auditing, organization
   development, condominium management, and highway
   maintenance

Personal services, for example, haircuts, personal banking, air
   conditioning repair, and child protection services

As you are aware, the Results Assessment System embraces results
in the domains of performance, learning, and perception outcomes.
Within the performance domain, it is important to be prepared for
the idea that a complex organization can have a variety of performance outcomes. Large or complex organizations often run subsystems as stand-alone organizations. For example, our guess is that the
manufacturing of Harley-Davidson motorcycles is very separate from
the Harley-Davidson clothing aspect of the total business. Furthermore, sometimes an organization that is a producer of goods will
have internal work groups that function as producers of internal services, and vice versa.

LEVELS OF SYSTEM OUTCOME
PERFORMANCE MEASURES

Performance outcomes are connected to the mission of the system.
Since there are so many varied systems in the world, the units of system outcomes are equally varied (for example, Ford Motor Company
makes cars, and the Union Gospel Mission saves souls). Sometimes
the milieux of potential performance outcomes from the varied systems are best classified in terms of the performance levels at the
whole system level (organization), the work processes within the system (subsystems), or the contributor level (individuals or intact work
groups).

   A simple example could revolve around fishing. Individual fishers could count the number of fish caught in a time period or the

The Million-Dollar Smile

We did some performance improvement consulting with a large regional health provider. We were asked to help assess the results from the execution of a companywide intervention to retain and gain customers who were flocking to competitors in response to inattentive treatment.

We found that the company decided to be nice to customers. All personnel, including the doctors, went through "nice training," and each clinic positioned a "nice person" at the entrance to greet and direct health care customers.

A number of decision makers at the health provider got infatuated with exploring the dimension of being nice. In identifying the performance outcome of "nice," all of us got temporarily sidetracked. Was it smiles? Emotional reactions? Time spent with patients? Then it hit us: the reason this was being done was to retain and gain customers. The system or mission-related outcome we were looking for was numbers of customers. The smiles turned into customers. Smiles were the drivers of performance in the system, not the performance outcomes. Each customer represented a modest annual profit that, when multiplied by the large number of new customers over the following sixteen months, could be converted to millions of dollars. From our experience with the "smile" variable, it had a direct and measurable impact on the core system performance outcome (the total number of people choosing the health provider as their health provider).

We recall the following candid statement by the president of Chrysler corporation: "Can you believe we are spending $60 million to teach our dealers to be nice to customers?" If their experience was like ours, there really are such things as million-dollar smiles!

number of fish that people in one boat caught. At the process level, the fishers could assess a new method of pulling in the catch and getting the fishing line set again. This would be assessed in terms of the percentage of time the line is in the water and the total fish caught during a time period compared to the old process. The fish market is a system that purchases fish from fishers, processes the different kinds of fish in various ways, and sells the fish. The market could assess performance outcomes for the day in terms of total pounds of fish sold, total dollar receipts, or the percentage profit margin for the day (considering the daily costs from the daily income).

Here are some additional sample measures of performance results in these three levels—system, work process, and group and individual. These levels and examples illustrate just a small portion of the range of mission-related performance outcomes among organizations. Each of the following examples is an expression of mission-related outcomes in a system context. Each can be financially analyzed quickly and valued in terms of financial results.

AETNA Insurance

System level: Total dollar worth of annual sales for the corporation (or division)

Work process level: Number of proposals submitted to clients by a regional office and approved through the proposal process

Individual or work group level: Number of clients retained by account managers

Ford Motor Company

System level: Number of cars sold in Europe

Work process level: Time to complete the final inspection process of the completed car at the end of the assembly line

Individual or work group level: Number of patents received by the engine fuel system research and development group

Union Gospel Mission

System level: Number of clients who are sober and self-supporting

Work process level: Number of meals served by the meal planning, preparation, and serving process

Individual or work group level: Number of people responding positively to the one-on-one-counseling intake program

CATEGORIES AND DIMENSIONS OF PERFORMANCE

The performance results require that a unit of performance be selected as the focal point of the assessment. It can be said that some clearly definable performance outcome is always present in any task, work group, work process, or organization. If a performance outcome cannot be identified, perhaps the intervention should not be implemented at all. Given the variety of organizations and their missions and goals, along with the levels at which interventions can be applied, there is almost no limit to the specific units of work performance or outcomes that could potentially be used. Everything, from lives saved, clients served, items produced, annual profit, and time to complete a project, shows up on the list. All of these situation-specific units of work performance can be identified initially as performance outcomes units of performance.

Performance outcomes can be assessed in terms of being counted or time taken to produce the units of goods or services. Performance drivers can also be thought of as quality features that are believed to have a direct impact on performance outcomes at a later time. Thus, the units, once identified, are named and then expressed in terms of *quantity, time*, or *quality features*. The assumption is that improvements in performance drivers will result in improvements of performance outcomes over time. In the interim, organizational decision makers will often place an estimated monetary value on performance driver data. In comparison, units of performance outcomes can be quantified and directly valued financially.

The familiar time dimension to performance is the time to produce a single unit or complete a single task or project. Time units may go as low as seconds and extend to months. The actual time interval will most commonly be in hours or days and will not likely exceed a week. Thus, you would indicate twenty days instead of four weeks, or forty hours instead of one week.

The familiar quantity dimension to performance is the number of things or tasks produced in a fixed period of time or the number of customers served. The time interval is most likely already specified in the work system. It could be as short term and concrete as having fifty computers assembled and packaged per eight-hour day. A longer term example would be having twelve active accounts at the end of a twelve-month period.

The quality features (or performance driver dimension) are more elusive. Performance drivers are the characteristics of the products or services produced or characteristics of the means of producing them that meet agreed-on specifications. Some of the product or service quality features fall in the realms of design, procurement, manufacturing, marketing, sales, service, customer education, and ultimate disposition (Tribus, 1985). The means of producing goods or services can be thought of as the performance variables or drivers.

The ultimate issue in the area of performance drivers is whether the organization is able to wait for the effects on performance outcomes (for example, putting out fifty computers per day with no defects versus putting out sixty computers—fifty with no defects and ten with defects). If the organization is not patient enough to wait for the quality intervention to take place in terms of core performance outcomes and for the financials to play out, organization decision makers are then responsible for saying, "I think that if we get this performance driver in place, it is worth so much money to the company" (for example, "every time we have a formal record indication of a dissatisfied customer, it costs us $500 in profit per year").

SALES COMMUNICATION CASE

The framing of the system and specifying the mission-related performance outputs in the sales communication case took some effort. First, the system was isolated to a major sector of the business: the sales of health care insurance in the corporation. Next, the performance outcomes were framed by the large account business (versus two other lines of business that have their own system, including their own sales force, management, and fiscal accountability).

Remember that the initial problem that the sales organization had identified was the lack of communication skills among sales personnel while closing the sale and lack of managerial support. The issues around this communication problem were quite compelling and temporarily distracted everyone into thinking that the outcome was improved communication (what we call a *performance driver*, not a *performance outcome*). In the end, the mission-related performance outcome of "sales" was (1) selected within the frame of the large account business segment or "system frame" of the corporation and (2) sales were confirmed to be the ultimate performance outcome expected from the sales communication improvement intervention.

MEASURING PERFORMANCE DRIVERS

So far we have talked about performance mostly as specific units of system outcomes, such as cars made or lawns mowed. And we have emphasized that every intervention should lead to system outcomes at some point. What we have not discussed yet are the situations where the near-term results of an intervention are not system outcomes but some other result that will lead to system outcomes at some point down the road. Consider the following examples:

- Learning organization interventions intended to enhance intellectual capital that will pay off with increased future performance
- Quality interventions that teach employees how to improve processes that will ultimately increase sales and market share
- Management development programs that prepare managers for future roles and retain high-potential employees

In these examples, it may be difficult to identify system outcomes expected to improve in the immediate future (say, thirty to ninety days) or less than a year. Yet they would be crucial to strengthening performance in the future. One criticism of results- or performance-oriented approaches to developing human resources is that they seem to value only interventions that produce short-term system performance outcomes. Nothing could be further from the truth.

The purpose here is to show how the Results Assessment System is also applied to the type of intervention that is called performance drivers (Holton, 1999; Kaplan and Norton, 1996). The Results Assessment System does pay special attention to the performance driver of learning. In many instances, learning can directly affect system outcomes by enabling people to do something they could not previously do. Our concern is how to deal with situations where the effect of the performance driver on system outcomes is not as immediate or occurs over an extended time.

Performance drivers are performance variables that are determined to sustain or increase system, subsystem, process, group, or individual performance in the future. Thus, they are *leading indicators* of future outcomes and tend to be unique for particular organizations.

Measuring performance drivers is of interest when it is clear from the up-front performance analysis that the performance driver is fully expected to produce performance outcomes. Performance drivers can be measured in the short term in anticipation that gains in the performance drivers will ultimately result in gains in performance outcomes to be assessed later.

Why Performance Drivers Matter

Outcome measures without performance drivers do not communicate how the outcomes are to be achieved. Conversely, performance drivers without outcome measures may enable the organization to achieve short-term operational improvements but will fail to reveal whether the operational improvements have been translated into expanded business. A good balanced scorecard should have an appropriate mix of outcomes (lagging indicators) and performance drivers (leading indicators) of the business unit's strategy (Kaplan and Norton, 1996, pp. 31–32).

From this perspective, improvement experts who focus solely on actual system performance outcomes, such as profit or units of work produced, are limited in that they are likely to focus on only short-term improvements and neglect aspects of the organization that will drive future performance outcomes. However, experts who focus solely on performance drivers such as learning or growth are equally limited in that they fail to consider the performance outcomes. When outcomes and drivers are appropriately linked and jointly considered, long-term performance improvement will likely occur.

Performance drivers are vital to organizational success. In fact, most HRD and other performance improvement interventions focus on some type of performance driver—for example, increasing employee motivation, improving morale, improving product quality, improving processes, and increasing employee suggestions. What all these have in common is that they may be vital to enhancing or maintaining system outcomes in the long run.

The Pattern of Effects

Fundamentally, all performance improvement and HRD practice operates on driver variables. Thus, performance drivers should predict future performance outcomes. Defining this pattern of effects is the job of up-front performance analysis and key to successful result assessment. The Performance Diagnosis Matrix (Figure 6.1) should substantively connect drivers of performance—the performance variables—to the performance goals.

The pattern of effects further defines the expected relationship between the performance driver and the performance outcome. For example, for a particular company, return on investment from sales might be an appropriate outcome measure that might be driven by customer loyalty and on-time delivery, and customer communication, which in turn might be driven by employee learning and internal process improvement efforts. The pattern could be portrayed like this:

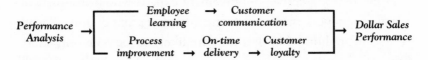

In the first part of this chapter we talked about system results in terms of performance outcomes—about connecting the performance analysis with the performance outcome. The performance outcome illustrated above is "sales performance in dollars." The performance analysis provided strong evidence that the performance drivers—the elements in the middle of the pattern of effects—will lead to the desired performance outcomes. Logically, then, it is important to assess the drivers while on the journey to performance outcomes to determine progress toward performance results. Be sure to remember that drivers are not performance outcomes; they are predictors of performance outcomes.

In a state government department of revenue, a performance outcome measure might be percentage of tax returns processed correctly

Figure 6.1. Performance Diagnosis Matrix of Enabling Questions

Performance Variables ↓

Performance Levels →

	Organization Level	Process Level	Individual Level
Mission/Goal	Does the organization mission or goal fit the reality of the economic, political, and cultural forces?	Do the process goals enable the organization to meet organization and individual missions or goals?	Are the professional and personal mission or goals of individuals congruent with the organization's?
System Design	Does the organization system provide structure and policies supporting the desired performance?	Are processes designed to work as a system?	Does the individual face obstacles that impede his or her job performance?
Capacity	Does the organization have the leadership, capital, and infrastructure to achieve its mission or goals?	Does the process have the capacity to perform (quantity, quality, and timeliness)?	Does the individual have the mental, physical, and emotional capacity to perform?
Motivation	Do the policies, culture, and reward systems support the desired performance?	Does the process provide the information and human factors required to maintain it?	Does the individual want to perform no matter what?
Expertise	Does the organization establish and maintain selection and training policies and resources?	Does the process of developing expertise meet the changing demands of changing processes?	Does the individual have the knowledge, skills, and experience to perform?

Source: Swanson, 1996.

within two weeks of receipt. A performance driver for that outcome might be the number of quality improvement initiatives successfully implemented as a result of quality improvement teams formed and the development of a leadership infrastructure. The pattern looks like this:

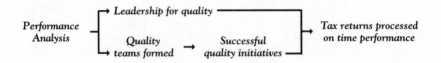

These performance outcome–performance driver examples point to several key conclusions:

- Every driver intervention has an assumed pattern of effect, although sometimes the exact form of the effects is not known until they occur.
- The pattern of effect may be unstated and untested, but it exists in someone's mind.
- Drivers have no inherent value to the organization, although they may be valuable to individuals or society (learning is an example).
- The value of drivers comes from the outcomes to which they contribute.
- Failure to define the pattern of effects breaks the link with organizational strategy.
- Without a defined pattern of effects, intermediate results are often mistaken for system outcomes.

Predicting System Outcomes from Driver Results

Often it is not acceptable to wait for actual outcomes to occur before producing system outcome results–assessment data and converting them to financial returns. In those cases, it is desirable to find ways to provide estimates of the likely payoff. The basic strategy is to find some way to calculate a formula by which driver results can be converted to likely system outcomes. Here are some commonly used techniques.

History. If the organization has had experience with a similar type of intervention, calculate the outcomes that occurred from them. For example, ABC Company, which is attempting a learning organization strategy, has applied for patents before and knows that it has been successful at converting 20 percent of its patents into marketable products.

Industry standards. Frequently industry trade groups maintain statistics about the payoff from an intervention. For example, most industrial groups know that every dollar invested in safety programs is likely to result in a certain percentage reduction in accident costs.

Benchmarking. In cases where competitive advantage is not at stake, it may be possible to consult similar other organizations to see what their experience has been. For example, a government department could benchmark with other similar government departments to estimate the extent to which quality improvement training is likely to result in improved services to citizens.

Trend lines. If an organization is in the middle of a multiyear intervention (such as quality or the learning organization), there may be a partial track record already established. In this case, a trend line could be plotted looking at the increase in performance outcomes from previous steps in the intervention.

Outside experts. Often outside experts know general formulas to predict outcomes from investments in performance drivers.

Consensus estimates. When no data are available, use the consensus estimates from a group of subject matter experts.

How to Select Performance Measures of System Outcomes

The worksheet shown in Figure 6.2 can be used to implement the ideas presented in this chapter. With practice, selecting performance measures of system outcomes should become quite easy.

CONCLUSIONS

Measuring performance results is critical to ultimate success. And the key to demonstrating performance results is being clear about the system: the mission of the system, the core goods or services outputs of the system, and connecting the intervention to these core outputs.

Most organizations have measures of their core system outputs already in place. The key for HRD professionals is to connect to the core performance outputs of the system or subsystem they are trying to improve. There are three ways to do this:

1. Conduct a front-end performance analysis that will dictate the performance opportunity, intervention, and performance outcome measures (see Swanson, 1996).
2. While working on the intervention without having completed an up-front performance analysis, simultaneously attempt to collect performance analysis data that will reshape the intervention and define the performance outcome measures.
3. After implementing an intervention not based on an up-front performance analysis, systematically raise the question of performance intent and search (more randomly) for performance outcomes attributable to the intervention. (Chapter Eleven explains this method, the Critical Outcome Technique.)

It is also critical to recognize the importance of performance drivers as being proxies of progress toward the journey to performance

Performance Results: Measuring System Outcomes

Figure 6.2. Performance Measure Worksheet

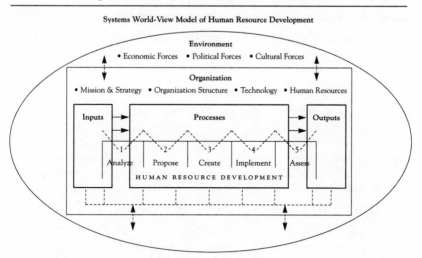

Systems World-View Model of Human Resource Development

1. Name of the organization (system or subsystem):
_____

2. Mission of the organization:
_____

3. If the framed system being assessed is not the organization above, specify one below:
___ Subsystem (name): _____
___ Work process (name): _____
___ Work group/job (name): _____

4. Mission-related unit of output performance for the framed system:
___ Good (name): _____ ___ Service (name): _____

5. Existing measure of mission-related units of output performance:
__ Quantity __Time __ Cost __ Quality feature (name): _____

6. If no measure of mission-related unit of output performance exists, establish by:

___ Top management (*meet with a person who oversees the system in terms of management or fiscal reporting to secure answer*)

___ Recognized expert (*meet with a person in system or in another similar system, or refer to industry standards to secure answer*)

___ Proposal from you (*take related pieces of the puzzle and put them together into a logical answer for management approval*)

7. Approval of measure of mission-related unit of output performance by the appropriate organizational decision maker in the organization.

outcomes. Assessing these elements provides valuable information about the progress being made within the performance driver realm until actual performance outcomes are assessed. (Chapter Fourteen presents a closer look at the issue of performance drivers.)

KEY POINTS TO REMEMBER

▼

- The development of strong, competitive, growing organizations requires an intense focus on performance results.
- Performance can be thought of as system results or financial results (or both).
- System results can be categorized as performance outcomes or performance drivers.
- Performance outcomes are units of output related to the system mission in the forms of goods or services.
- Measures of performance outcomes can be at three levels: system, work process, and group or individual.
- Units of performance outcomes are expressed in terms of quantity, time, or quality features.
- Performance drivers are variables that are related to and enable performance outcomes.

7

Performance Results
Measuring Financial Outcomes

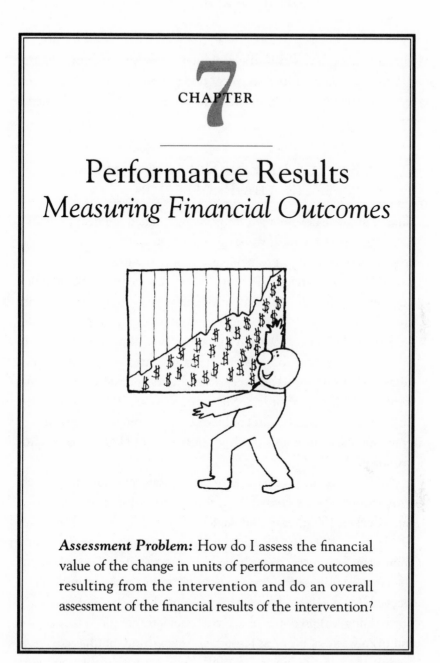

Assessment Problem: How do I assess the financial value of the change in units of performance outcomes resulting from the intervention and do an overall assessment of the financial results of the intervention?

▼

The second option within the performance results domain is financial results, defined as the conversion of the output units of goods or services attributable to the intervention into money and financial interpretation.

STATUS OF FINANCIAL ANALYSIS IN THE PROFESSION

Human resource development professionals, like other decision makers in organizations, must work up budgets, justify their own salaries, propose strategies and projects, and report the financial results of programs to top management. Yet a recent study of professional practices reports that only 3 percent of the development programs in organizations are evaluated in terms of financial impact (Bassi, Benson, and Cheney, 1996). This is true even though the research clearly demonstrates that systematic interventions focused on performance through HRD deliver an eight-to-one return on investment (ROI) in a year or less. Managers who are skeptical that the ROI is this high can be directed to a recent summary of fifteen relevant such studies about the high potential of HRD investments (Swanson, 1998).

Organizations are economic entities, and they ultimately judge each of their components from an ROI framework, with or without valid data (Becker, 1993; Dean and Ripley, 1997; Edvinsson and Malone, 1997; Ulrich, 1997). To face this challenge, four views of performance improvement interventions have been presented to the profession: (1) a major business process—something an organization must do to succeed, (2) a value-added activity—something that is potentially worth doing, (3) an optional activity—something that is nice to do, and (4) a waste of business resources—something that has costs exceeding the benefits (Swanson, 1995). Unfortunately, the dominant view of HRD is that of being an optional activity having costs greater than its benefits. The idea that HRD is overhead, and not generally a good investment, is popular and entrenched among organizational decision makers. The irony is that the profession's widely known four-level evaluation model lacks both the underlying economic principles and practical tools required to get to reporting financial results.

ASSESSING FINANCIAL RESULTS: THE MODEL AND METHOD

The model and method for determining the financial ROI of an HRD effort are relatively simple and straightforward in terms of actual and forecasted benefits. Both have three main components: (1) performance value resulting from the program, (2) cost of the program, and (3) benefit resulting from the program (Swanson and Gradous, 1988). The basic financial results model is: Performance value – Cost = Benefit.

The assessment method is an expansion of the three model components into three separate worksheets plus a "thinking sheet" in the form of a time-performance graph. The discussion that follows explains the financial analysis method in the context of the sales communication case. First we review the case from the system results and then the financial result perspectives.

For the system results, the decision was to measure sales that were attributed to individuals and to do this sixty days following the training portion of the intervention. In this case, sales personnel make a small number of sales that are individually worth a great deal. The sixty days were needed in order to determine the effect, if any, that the communication intervention had on sales.

For the financial results, the total number of sales was multiplied by the net worth of an average sale: $120,000. A meeting with the comptroller yielded this figure following a conversation about available financial data. The direct cost of the program is compared to the net profit from the reported sales attributable to sales communication project to determine the financial return.

Time-Performance Graph

The time-performance graph helps visualize the performance financial analysis method (Figure 7.1). The vertical axis registers performance levels in terms of performance units at both the beginning and end of the program for each option being considered. The horizontal axis is the length of time to reach the performance goal for each option being considered.

Figure 7.1 illustrates the comparison of two options and a performance level greater than zero. Option 2, a structured intervention (systematically executed), is visually compared to option 1, an unstructured intervention (as is, trial and error, or on the job). According to the figure, if the structured option is chosen, the individual or work group performance goal is reached much faster than if the unstructured option is chosen. In this instance, the added performance wedge between the option 1 and option 2 is the added value resulting from the program. If the unstructured option had no direct costs and the structured option had costs, these costs are subtracted from the performance values to determine the financial benefits.

Figure 7.2 illustrates the time-performance graph for the sales communication case study. It shows that the performance goal increases and the time to reach the goal decreases. Both have performance consequences in terms of system results and financial results.

Performance Value Worksheet

The performance value is the financial worth of the number of performance units that result from an intervention. It is calculated by multiplying the total number of units of performance expected to

Figure 7.1. Time-Performance Graph Comparing Two Options

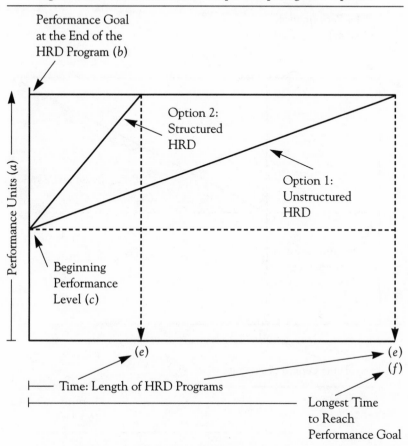

result from the program times the dollar value of one unit. Figure 7.3 is the worksheet for the sales communication case.

Cost Worksheet

A program cost is any expenditure that the organization chooses to attribute to the program. An intervention cost in one organization may not necessarily be a program cost in another. It is important that professionals account for costs in the same manner as the organization

Figure 7.2. Time-Performance Graph for the Communication Case Study

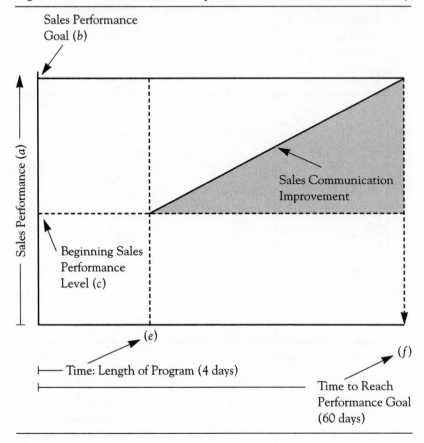

does and that these practices remain constant from assessment to assessment. To ensure this, the financial result method allows assessors to customize the cost analysis worksheet to include the established cost categories of the organization (for example, salary, equipment, and supplies) and the HRD process phases (analyze, propose, create, implement, and assess). The generic worksheet shown in Figure 7.4 can be used as is or can be customized for a particular organization.

The Magic Number

It was about 4:00 p.m. on a Thursday, and we were getting ready to call it a day when the office phone rang. It was a call from Onan Corporation across town. Onan's HRD and plant production staff were trying to apply the financial result model to a performance improvement program. The program involved the addition of high-tech machining centers and training workers to operate them. They were stuck in their financial analysis and wanted some advice. We agreed to drive right over to meet with them.

Once we arrived, we probed as to the original problem and the original goal. The answers were quite vague—something about the need for new technology and increased productivity; nothing specific or useful came out. They did know how much the equipment cost and how much it was going to cost to train the people. Finally, one of us asked, "Who made the decision to buy this equipment?" It was the vice president of manufacturing. Call him, we demanded. Within a few minutes of conversation with him, the magic number came out: each of those machining centers had the capability of producing $550 of product per hour. That was the magic number that drove Onan to buy them in the first place and the magic number needed to put the cost of the operator training into economic perspective.

Benefit Worksheet

The benefit computation is a simple subtraction activity recorded on the benefit worksheet (Figure 7.5). The costs are subtracted from their performance values to obtain the benefits. Any reasonable option should forecast a positive benefit. The optimal financial benefit is the one with the highest benefit.

DEVELOPING MEASURES OF RESULTS

Figure 7.3. Performance Value Worksheet

Note that performance units and time units for all options *must remain consistent* throughout the assessment.

Program _____   Analyst _____   Date _____

Option name   1. _____   2. _____

Date required for calculations:

(a) What unit of work
performance are you   _____   _____
measuring?   unit name   unit name

(b) What is the performance
goal per worker/work   ___ ___ / ___   ___ ___ / ___
group at the end of the no. units / time no. units / time
HRD program?

(c) What is the performance
per worker/work group   ___ ___ / ___   ___ ___ / ___
at the beginning of the no. units / time no. units / time
HRD program?

(d) What dollar value is $ _____ / unit $ _____ / unit
assigned to each
performance unit?

(e) What is the development
time required to   ___ ___   ___ ___
reach the expected   no. time   no. time
performance level?

(f) What is the evaluation
period? (Enter the longest ___ ___   ___ ___
time (e) of all options   no. time   no. time
being considered.)

(g) How many workers/work
groups will participate in _____   _____
the HRD program?   no. workers/groups   no. workers/groups

Figure 7.3. Performance Value Worksheet, Cont'd.

Calculations to determine net performance value:

(h) Will worker/work group
produce usable units during   ___no.___ ___units___   ___no.___ ___units___
the HRD program? If no,
enter 0. If yes, enter known
performance rate or calcu-
late average performance
rate. [(b + c)/2]

(i) What total units per
worker/work group will be   ___no. of units___   ___no. of units___
produced during the devel-
opment time? (h x e)

(j) How many units will be
produced per worker/work   ___no. of units___   ___no. of units___
group during the evaluation
period? {[(f − e) x b] + i}

(k) What will be the value of $ _____ $ _____
the worker's/work group's
performance during the
evaluation period? (j x d)

(l) What is the performance $ _____ $ _____
value gain per worker/
work group? [k − (c x d x f)]

(m) What is the total perfor- $ _____ $ _____
mance value gain for all   Option 1   Option 2
workers/work groups? (l x g)

Figure 7.4. Cost Analysis Worksheet

Program _____   Analyst _____   Date _____

Option name	1 _____	2 _____
Analyze		
Diagnose performance requirements	_____	_____
Document learning requirements	_____	_____
Other _____	_____	_____
Other _____	_____	_____
Propose		
Intervention design	_____	_____
Detailed program design	_____	_____
Other _____	_____	_____
Other _____	_____	_____
Create		
Leader materials	_____	_____
Participant materials	_____	_____
Other _____	_____	_____
Other _____	_____	_____
Implement		
Program management	_____	_____
Program delivery	_____	_____
Other _____	_____	_____
Other _____	_____	_____
Assess		
Assess outcomes	_____	_____
Report results	_____	_____
Other _____	_____	_____
Other _____	_____	_____
Total HRD program costs	$ _____ (Option 1)	$ _____ (Option 2)

Figure 7.5. Benefits Analysis Worksheet

Program _____	Analyst _____	Date _____
Option name	1_____	2 _____
Performance Value	$_____	$ _____
Minus Cost	_____	_____
Benefits	$_____	$ _____

Note: Circle your choice of option.

COACHING INTERVENTION FINANCIAL OUTCOMES

The following case illustrates the forecasting of financial performance results. This intervention, like most others, involves multiple performance variables or performance drivers. It focused on the need for expertise among workers and supervisors, and a change in the job requirements among supervisors to include coaching. The same forms can also be used to record actual financial outcomes.

The Situation

The manager of a government auditing and collection agency regularly puts groups of new recruits through a 240-hour training course before sending them off to work in the field. The course was, however, just the beginning of their training. On average, an additional fifteen months of on-the-job experience are required for the new staff to become competent. Believing that the time to reach full performance could be shortened, the internal performance consultant gathered a committee of eight experts to discuss the situation and to devise a plan for accelerating learning on the job. The strategy was simple: teach the experienced staff how to be more effective coaches of the new staff and provide the incentive for them to follow through.

After exploring several alternative packages for developing coaching skills in supervisors, the committee settled on the option of asking the National Association of Auditors to conduct a four-day training program for ten experienced staff who are now expected to coach one new worker as part of each of their supervisory responsibilities. This option was then compared to the current, more leisurely method of gaining full competency from the workers.

The committee asked the performance consultant to forecast the ROI of the project and to include the committee's work in the project's costs. Establishing the unit of performance as a "collection" and the dollar worth of each collection per hour having a performance standard of $175 of collections per hour required a consensus decision on the part of several top managers.

Performance Valuing of the Coaching Program

Forecasting the new performance value in this case presents an obstacle worth noting. The unit of performance was rather arbitrarily determined. An auditor-collector works with a number of clients who have extremely diverse characteristics. Thus, one client's work could take many days to process, while another's could be processed in a few hours. Clients' personalities and the variety of their economic endeavors confound the issue of finding an appropriate unit of performance. Finally, however, dollars collected was established as the primary performance unit for purposes of the forecast. Past records of exemplary, average, and below-average performers provided the basis for setting an average of $175 in identified collections per hour as the primary performance goal of the development program. In fact, these average numbers are regularly monitored and reported as a means of tracking and evaluating work groups and individuals. The average figures also accommodated all the types and sizes of clients that any one auditor-collector could be expected to work with over a period of time.

Clearly, one could be genuinely concerned that the unit of performance set for purposes of the forecast is carried into the trainee's workplace as the single measure of quality work performance. This would be inappropriate. The measure does have great utility in forecasting, but it may also distort performance in the workplace over time. Finding a single simple measure of performance for a previously undefined job has the potential of intoxicating managers with ideas of "control." Such quantity-only goals could end up encouraging dishonesty and the leveraging of "profitable" clients, and result in generally poor customer service in the workplace. This is where the discussion of pattern of effects helps make sure that the focus of the performance drivers is not lost in pursuit of the performance outcomes. The completed performance value forecast is presented in Figure 7.6.

Cost Analysis of the Coaching Case

The cost worksheet for the coaching skills program is shown in Figure 7.7. Note that this sheet was customized to match this organization's training process model phases of analyze, design, develop, implement, and evaluate. It is important to note that this organization, like most other organizations, has accounting systems in place and that costs are almost always systematically accounted for. The internal HRD consultant estimated the costs of the program in making her proposal for the project.

The expenses of the committee would primarily fall within this phase. A check of wage classifications and rates showed that, on average, each committee member's salary amounted to $15.00 per hour. With benefits added, the cost of each member's time was calculated to be about $20.60 per hour. The committee planned to meet about five times for four hours each time. Committee time for

Figure 7.6. Performance Value Worksheet

Note that performance units and time units for all options *must remain consistent* throughout the assessment.

Program ___Coaching Skills___   Analyst ___C. Sleezer___   Date _____

Option name   1. ___Unstructured___   2. ___NAA Course___

Date required for calculations:

(a) What unit of work performance are you measuring?

     Dollar ($) — unit name   *Dollar ($)* — unit name

(b) What is the performance goal per worker/work group at the end of the HRD program?

175	$	/ Hr.		175	$	/ Hr.
no.	units	/ time		no.	units	/ time

(c) What is the performance per worker/work group at the beginning of the HRD program?

0	$	/ hr.		0	$	/ Hr.
no.	units	/ time		no.	units	/ time

(d) What dollar value is assigned to each performance unit?

     $ _1_ / unit $ _1_ / unit

(e) What is the development time required to reach the expected performance level?

2625	Hrs.		2250	Hrs.
no.	time		no.	time

(f) What is the evaluation period? (Enter the longest time (e) of all options being considered.)

2625	Hrs.		2625	Hrs.
no.	time		no.	time

(g) How many workers/work groups will participate in the HRD program?

     10 — no. workers/groups   10 — no. workers/groups

Performance Results: Measuring Financial Outcomes

Figure 7.6. Performance Value Worksheet, Cont'd.

Calculations to determine net performance value:

(h) Will worker/work group produce usable units during the HRD program? If no, enter 0. If yes, enter known performance rate or calculate average performance rate. [(b + c)/2]

87	$	87	$
no.	units	no.	units

(i) What total units per worker/work group will be produced during the development time? (h x e)

228,375	195,750
no. of units	no. of units

(j) How many units will be produced per worker/work group during the evaluation period? {[(f – e) x b] + i}

228,375	261,375
no. of units	no. of units

(k) What will be the value of the worker's/work group's performance during the evaluation period? (j x d)

$ ___228,375___ $ ___261,375___

(l) What is the performance value gain per worker/work group? [k – (c x d x f)]

$ ___228,375___ $ ___261,375___

(m) What is the total performance value gain for all workers/work groups? (l x g)

$	2,283,750	$	2,613,750
	Option 1		Option 2

**Figure 7.7. Cost Analysis Worksheet
for the Government Auditing and Collection Agency**

Program _Coaching Skills_   Analyst _C. Jones_   Date _____

Option name	1 Unstructured	2 NAA Course
Analyze		
Diagnose performance requirements		3,296
Document learning requirements		
Other _(tuition and time)_		680
Other _(proposal costs)_		70
Propose		
Intervention design		412
Detailed program design		
Other _____		
Other _____		
Create		
Leader materials		280
Participant materials		
Other _(HRD manager)_		82
Other _____		
Implement		
Program management		
Program delivery		3,000
Other _(HRD manager)_		
Other _____		164
Assess		
Assess outcomes		989
Report results		
Other _(secretarial)_		42
Other _____		
Total HRD program costs	$ _____ (Option 1)	$ _47,415_ (Option 2)

the project would total $3,296.00 ($20.60 per hour × 4 hours × 5 meetings × 8 members). No food or travel costs for committee members would be charged to the program.

Two of the committee members planned to prepare for the work of the committee by meeting with a class at a local college to study effective coaching. Eight hours of class time and a tuition fee of $175.00 for each totaled about $680.00 [($20.60 per hour × 8 hours × 2 members + $175.00 tuition fee × 2 members)].

Writing the performance improvement proposal to the director of the agency was to be done in committee sessions, but typing the proposal would require the skills of a secretary. Secretarial time was valued at $10.60 per hour, including benefits. Five hours would be needed to type, duplicate, and distribute the proposal to management. Total secretarial and duplication costs were forecast to be about $70.00 [($10.60 per hour × 5 hours + $17.00 duplication cost].

Propose The major expense of this phase would be incurred in changing some of the language of the presenter's script and the case studies and altering other small procedural details of the NAA's usual coaching skills program. Two people working about ten hours would be needed to customize the program, and this would cost $412.00 ($20.60 per hour × 10 hours × 2 staff).

Create The major expense for this phase would be for typing and duplicating a customized coaching manual (for each of the twelve participants) at a cost of $20.00 per manual. The forecast total for this phase is $280.00 [($20.00 per manual × 10 coaches) + 4 extra].

About four hours of the HRD manager's time would be needed to telephone each of the ten participants to prepare them to attend the session. The telephone time would be used to discuss any concerns that the manager-coaches might have. This time was forecast to cost about $82.00 ($20.60 per hour × 4 hours).

Implement The HRD manager planned to spend one-half day briefing the ten coaches before turning them over to the NAA trainer. This half-day would be followed by three days of customized training. After the training, the performance consultant again planned to spend a half-day with the participating coaches, this time in a debriefing session. (The cost of the coaches' lost productivity for four days and the performance consultant's time for one day would be included in the cost forecast. The NAA trainer's time would be included in the fee to be paid to the NAA for the entire course.) The performance consultant's time for one day of meeting with the coaches was expected to cost about $164.00 ($20.60 per hour × 8 hours).

The performance consultant believed that the coaches' productivity would drop about 50 percent during the four days of training. The drop was not forecast at $240 per hour (full rate) because the coaches would presumably have projects in motion, and problems with these projects could be handled by telephone as needed during the four days they would be off the job. One of the committee members who was planning to attend the training as a coach verified this presumption. The lost productivity would amount to $38,400 ($120 per hour × 8 hours × 4 days × 10 coaches).

A call to the NAA established that the fee to be paid to it as compensation for the use of one trainer for three days and for the original course content would be roughly $1,000 per day, for a total of $3,000. No travel or food expenses were expected or forecast.

Assess The HRD manager believed that two government evaluators would spend three days in monitoring the training, assessing the results, and reporting to the agency director. Their time for assessment and reporting would amount to just under $989.00 ($20.60 per hour × 8 hours × 3 days × 2 trainers).

Typing, duplicating, and distributing the evaluation report were expected to take three hours of secretarial time, or about $32.00

($10.60 per hour × 3 hours). Duplicating the report was expected to cost another $10.00, for a total of $42.00.

Cost Decisions Perhaps not perfectly obvious are two decisions that were made to ensure that costs were not unnecessarily overstated. The first decision was not to estimate the cost of the meeting room where the program would be delivered. It is the site for all regular meetings of the collection staff, and no differentiation is made among the variety of activities held there. The second, and more crucial, decision was to charge to the program 50 percent of the coaches' lost productivity during their time in the program. The coaches' salaries while in training were easily covered by the 50 percent of their productivity not charged to the program. Charging for time lost and productivity lost would have overstated the cost of the program.

Benefit Analysis Decisions

Remember that this public sector case describes an auditing and collection agency whose new staff had previously required fifteen months of field experience to reach competency. A program to teach coaching skills to experienced staff to use when working with the new staff was determined to be an appropriate method for shortening the process of developing new staff. The forecaster looked at two options: the existing fifteen-month development program and a new thirteen-month structured option. Figure 7.8 presents the benefit analysis for both programs. From a strictly financial perspective, the structured program would appear to be by far the more desirable: $2,566,335 in benefit versus only $2,283,750 for the existing program. The other five decision criteria of appropriateness, availability, quality, prior effectiveness, and cost would also need to be applied before recommending a program choice to decision makers. In this instance, the

**Figure 7.8. Benefit Design Worksheet
for the Government Auditing and Collection Agency**

Program _Coaching Skills_	Analyst _C. Jones_	Date _____

	Option name	1 _Unstructured_	2 _NAA Course_
Performance Value		$ 2,283,750	$ 2,613,750
Minus Cost		0	47,415
Benefits		$ 2,283,750	$ (2,566,335)

Note: Circle your choice of option.

up-front cost of the program with the higher benefit was the only serious consideration. The agency was on a fixed budget and would have to make an appeal to a special government agency to fund this effort. Nevertheless, the new coaching program was supported by the decision makers because of its forecast benefit. An assessment following the program would collect actual data using the same financial model and forms for reporting the actual results.

FINANCIAL ANALYSIS AS AN ELEMENT OF DECISION MAKING AND ACCOUNTABILITY

For many HRD professionals, talking about their work in financial terms is new. The financial results model and method we have presented has worked time and time again. In the assessment of financial results, placing a dollar value on the unit of performance can be a stumbling block in the beginning. Here are suggestions in determining the unit value, the magic number:

- Express the units of performance in positive numbers (for example, refer to the 80 percent retention of managers rather than the 20 percent turnover of managers).

- In locating the person with the "magic number," think of the person who is being held fiscally accountable for the system or work group in question.
- Locate the credible person in the organization that has the "magic number" (the worth of the unit of performance). Use that number as well as the credibility of the person who provided it in reporting the results.

Financial benefit is only one criterion for choosing or supporting a particular HRD programs or programs option. There are four additional useful criteria to use when thinking about why people choose and support interventions in addition to the financial benefit to the organization:

- Appropriateness to the organizational culture and tradition
- Quality features of the program
- Effectiveness of the program
- Cost of the program

The nonfinancial criteria in this list cannot be ignored. Organizations are not totally rational and certainly are not totally directed by economics. For example, a program forecasting high financial benefit that flies in the face of the organizational culture and tradition will never likely get off the ground or sustain continuing support.

CONCLUSION

When HRD professionals are able to present financial results data with assurance, they increase the odds that their contributions to the improvement of the organization will be accepted and realized. Being able to report financial results is dependent on the ability to specify system results. Perhaps even more important is the ability to forecast financial outcomes so as to gain organization approval of HRD investments. The financial model is the same for both fore-casting financial benefits and assessing financial benefits after the fact. Forecasts require dollar estimates, while results assessments track the actual dollars.

KEY POINTS TO REMEMBER

▼

- Performance results can be categorized as system results or financial results.
- Financial results are the conversion of the output units of goods or services attributable to the intervention into money and financial interpretation.
- The financial results model is: Performance value − Cost = Benefit.
- Systematically designed and implemented HRD efforts based on sound analysis consistently yield an ROI of two to one or greater in a year or less.
- Human resource development professionals have tools available to assess and forecast the financial returns on HRD development efforts.

8

Learning Results

Measuring Knowledge and Expertise Outcomes

Assessment Problem: How do I create or select good measures of learning? More specifically, how do I select or develop learning measures of knowledge and expertise?

▼

Within the Results Assessment System, learning results are classified into knowledge and expertise. Knowledge results are defined as mental achievements acquired through study and experience. Expertise results are defined as human behaviors having effective results and optimal efficiency acquired through study and experience within a specialized domain.

All organizations rely on human knowledge and expertise in order to establish and achieve their goals. Thus, the concern for learning is fundamental. HRD professionals and organizational leaders should not waiver on this fact. People need to know and to be able to do things in order to perform. Yet just because they know and are able to do things does not mean they will perform in those arenas. Although knowledge and expertise are critical prerequisites to performance, they can be blocked from being utilized (for example, by not providing people with the needed tools or questioning or ridiculing people for trying new techniques).

Learning and the verification of learning matters to organizations and to the HRD profession. There is no substitute for the direct assessment of knowledge and expertise. Yet HRD professionals widely hold two beliefs that are refuted by the research and are counterproductive when it comes to assessing learning results: (1) that high positive participant reactions to learning experience are related to actual learning and (2) that anyone can learn anything.

Both of these false beliefs tend to support each other and end up implying that learning experiences should not make the learner uncomfortable through either the design of the experience or the assessment of the learning results. Fortunately, organizations and the individuals who work in them continuously sort themselves out in terms of interests and capacity. The reality is that adult learners are not fragile, adults almost always get into jobs that match their capacity and interests, and workers expect that they must perform and demonstrate their knowledge and expertise. Learning results are expected (and probable) after people attend development sessions, but you do not know if they have gained the needed knowledge or expertise without an assessment.

This discussion may sound inconsistent with adult learning theories that focus on the learner, but it is not. There are severe limitations to learners' controlling all of their own learning process (see Knowles, Holton, and Swanson, 1998). The need for focus and control is one reason that the HRD profession exists in the first place. Formative evaluation as part of the active learning experience—assessment that gives in-process diagnosis, feedback, and direction—is very much a part of sound adult learning theory and good HRD practice. In-process formative evaluation may at times resemble the assessment of results, but its purpose and how it is handled are fundamentally different. For example, an instructor could use a knowledge test as an in-process part of the learning experience that looks similar to the summative test of knowledge results that is used to verify if participants learned the material. The instructor could ask the participants to work in pairs to provide their initial answers to the formative test items and to confirm them from the supporting training materials. This is a good learning strategy and a bad result assessment. From an adult learning theory perspective, the formative test guides and supports the learner through the learning process. From an HRD theory perspective and its concern about results, the instructor and the sponsoring organization still have no idea how much each participant knows unless a test of knowledge results is administered to each participant.

The most unique and attainable result contribution HRD can make is to deliver confirmed learning outcomes consistently. Nevertheless, it is important to remember that individuals cannot accurately self-rate their learning, and even if learning (in the forms of knowledge and expertise) has been achieved, there is another whole set of workplace conditions required to unleash that learning in the organization.

Learning Hurts

Ben Franklin succinctly informed us over two hundred years ago that "learning hurts." As a Renaissance man and joyful learner, Franklin could not have meant pain and punishment. Rather, he meant the hard work of hard thinking, casting off the comfortable old ideas, and breaking in the not-so-comfortable new ones. He wisely knew that learning is a serious journey and not the same as an amusement event. In assessing learning results, most of us would probably say that we do not like taking tests. But we surely want our airplane pilots, heart surgeons, retirement account managers, theologians, and automobile brake system mechanics to have passed their tests. In the same manner, organizations and individuals should want evidence of the required knowledge and expertise to succeed.

Several years ago we put on a three-day performance improvement seminar to a group of top executives of a Fortune 500 company. They were assigned to read a book prior to the seminar so as to save time and to level out the knowledge starting point of the group. When they were given the book, they were informed that the first activity of the seminar was going to be a pretest on its content. As the paper-and-pencil multiple-choice test was passed out at the beginning of the seminar, one of the executives announced that he did not like the requirement of having to take a test. When asked why, he said, "Because it made me read the book." Everyone in the class looked at each other and smiled—even the executive who offered the comment. Ben Franklin would have smiled too.

Assessment of learning results requires organizations and individuals to specify the knowledge and expertise required to sustain themselves and then advance. This chapter provides numerous practical and theoretically sound ways to construct measures of knowledge and expertise.

GOOD TESTS—BAD TESTS

Professionals in the business of developing good measurement devices are focused on the reliability and validity of measurement instruments. A reliable instrument yields consistent results. For example, step on the bathroom scale, and it reads 157 pounds. Step off and step back on, and it now reads 184 pounds. This is not a reliable, let alone accurate, instrument. And unless an explanation or a quick fix emerges, the bathroom scale will be thrown in the trash or taken back to the store for a refund.

How much do you weigh? You still do not know. Try this example: you get on your bathroom scale, and it reads 184 pounds; then you get off and on again for a second reading of 184. Given these consistent results, it is reasonable to say that the bathroom scale is reliable. That is good. But how much do you weigh? A valid instrument accurately measures what it purports to measure. Your best estimate is that you weigh 184 pounds, but is that accurate? Suppose you have a second weight scale, and you get on and off both scales several times, taking readings as you go. Your original bathroom scale continues to read 184 reliably. The second scale reliably reads 179. Both scales are reliable, and both purport to measure your weight. Which do you believe? At this point all that can be said is that neither scale is accurate or valid. To get help in clarifying which is accurate—the validity question—you could find a third scale purporting to measure weight or obtain additional information about the quality of the existing two scales. What if the second scale used was a large commercial counterbalance scale at a doctor's office and the first bathroom scale was a ten dollar spring-action item from a discount store? The credibility of the second scale would allow you to accept the 179 pound number. And you probably would adjust the ten dollar bathroom scale to read 179 pounds. Once recalibrated, the bathroom scale could then be thought of as being reliable and valid.

Content Validity

Reliability and validity are basic to thinking about, developing, and selecting instruments, and we will use them as a basis for the later sections on measuring knowledge and expertise results. But there is a core issue related to establishing the integrity of an instrument: content validity, that is, the degree to which the instrument content matches the desired content. Establishing and confirming content validity of an instrument is the most critical factor in establishing measures of learning. Getting the wrong sample of content is disastrous in terms of assessing results. A test has content validity if it has a representative sample of all the content being considered.

The two general bases for content validity are the structure of the work or the structure of the subject matter. For example, for a financial analyst, the structure that comes from the flow of her work tasks and work processes is quite different from the structure derived from the economic and investment bodies of knowledge. A choice must be made as to which option is (or whether both options are) critical to the mission of the organization and the expectations placed on the individual contributors. Human resource professionals interested in selection and competence more often focus on the structure of the subject matter, while those interested in expertise and performance focus on the work process and tasks. Clearly there is significant overlap between both approaches and significant differences.

How to Build in Content Validity and Reliability

The content validity of a test can be achieved by using a content validity matrix, like that in Figure 8.1. The vertical axis of the matrix is a breakdown of the units of content directly derived from the content analysis: the structure of the work or the subject matter. The horizontal axis segments the units of content into two levels of complexity: lower or higher level content. Cognitive lower knowledge test items can be thought of as requiring a person to recall basic information such as names, facts, and elements. Cognitive higher knowledge test items require a person to have basic information and to think beyond the recall of information to applying it, using it to analyze a situation, and using the new knowledge to judge the value of something. The percentage weighting of the rows and cells as to their relative worth and specifying the actual numbers of test items in each is critical. It ensures that the test profile matches the knowledge demands determined through the analysis.

The following two guidelines are important to the development of the content validity matrix:

Figure 8.1. Sample Content Validity Matrix

Knowledge Level of Items → *Content of Test*	*Cognitive Lower* *Test Items* *(recall)* *Number/Percent*		*Cognitive Higher* *Test Items* *(applying)* *Number/Percent*		*Totals* *Test Items* *Number/Percent*	
Unit 1 (name)	6	15	6	15	12	30
Unit 2 (name)	4	10	2	5	6	15
Unit 3 (name)	3	7.5	5	12.5	8	20
Unit 4 (name)	7	17.5	7	17.5	14	35
Totals (of test items)	20	50%	20	50%	40	100%

1. Make sure that the profile of the measure of knowledge matches the content required or taught and its relative emphasis. The knowledge content should be organized by the structure of the work process and tasks, the structure of the subject matter, or both.
2. Use a matrix with the content breakdown on one axis. Use cognitive-lower and cognitive-higher knowledge levels on the other axis. Weight the percentage distribution of test items according to the learner's time on task or relative importance.

The idea of starting to plan for a learning experience and a measurement instrument by writing learning objectives is appropriate for schooling, but is not a logical starting point for assessing learning results in organizations. The thorough up-front analysis of the performance and work behavior requirements and relevant subject matter analysis is the ideal basis for designing learning and measures of learning (see Swanson, 1996). It is here that you identify the content of the program and the test. This analysis then can be easily converted into the units of content portrayed in the content validity matrix, their relative importance, and the relative cognitive higher cognitive lower emphasis.

Learning objectives are useful means of articulating this same information to learners without all the detail required for planning. Good learning objectives meet three criteria:

1. Learner behavior outcome (what the learner, not the instructor, must know or do)
2. Standards (quantity, time, or quality features of the outcomes)
3. Conditions (context and conditions of the demonstration of learning)

The solution to building reliability into a test is quite simple if this rule is followed: the more test items (or observations) there are, the more reliable the test is. The common five- to ten-item test will almost always have highly questionable reliability. As a generalization, twenty items or more is minimal. We have found that sixty-item tests are almost always highly reliable but push the upper limits of test length in organizations. Although the actual reliability can be calculated after the test has been given and the data analyzed, you want to build in reliability from the start. To do so, it is important to have a large enough sample of items.

Here is what happens when you do not have enough test items: Suppose you knew quite a bit about a topic, but the test of your knowledge was a single question. If you did not know the answer to that one question, you would be judged a failure. And somebody who knows much less generally might know that particular answer and be rated high. Increase the number of items to five, and this would less likely happen, and so on as the number of test items increases.

Clearly there can be conflict between the need for a learning result assessment and the amount of time available for assessment versus the entire learning experience itself. One solution is to provide smaller tests for each segment of the learning experience, to spread them throughout the experience, and to combine the scores for one total test score. For example, a four-day seminar we delivered to a corporate management group had five units of content. We gave five fifteen-item multiple-choice tests, one at the end of each unit of learning, and combined all the scores at the end of the seminar for the final score on the seventy-five-item test. A carefully written seventy-five-item multiple-choice test will almost always have very high reliability. And if the test was based on a content validity matrix, the odds are that you have built a test with high content validity and reliability.

DEVELOPING MEASURES OF KNOWLEDGE

Knowledge, an intellectual or cognitive result of learning experiences, is the basic learning result. It is lodged in a person's mind.

Measures of knowledge confirm the level of knowledge held by individuals within a particular subject area. In terms of being both effective and efficient, paper-and-pencil tests of knowledge are the primary means of measuring knowledge.

Measures of knowledge and the structure of the questions can take many forms. Here are some of the wide range of alternatives. Remember that our approach is in search of the practical, while being credible in terms of producing valid data.

Developing Test Items

There are numerous types of test items, and most people have their biases about them and tests in general. Some of the groundless biases go like this: "You can't measure what I know from a test." "I can't take tests." "Only essay tests get at the important information." We could go on with this, but our goal is to simplify the development of measures while maintaining assessment integrity. To accomplish this, all test items can be limited to two types: multiple-choice questions and matching questions. Both types of questions allow you to achieve four good outcomes:

1. Maximize the number of test items.
2. Get the most data in the least amount of time.
3. Measure cognitive-higher and cognitive-lower knowledge.
4. Be able to score the tests accurately in the least amount of time.

The decision to use multiple-choice versus matching test items is based on fit and variety. Most content more easily fits multiple choice, so when the content more easily fits the matching format, we suggest using it. And we suggest using both formats to create variety for the person taking the test.

Never use true-false items because a person has a 50 percent chance of getting the item correct without knowing anything. And by sticking to two types of questions, you get more efficient at developing good measures of knowledge results.

Developing Multiple-Choice Test Items Here is a good multiple-choice test item. Begin by noting that there are two essential parts, the stem and the alternatives:

The levels of performance, as presented in this seminar, are:
_____ A. organizational, task, and individual.
_____ B. job description, task inventory, and task analysis.
_____ C. organizational, work process, and group process.
___X___ D. organizational, process, and individual.

This is a cognitive-lower item. It asks the test taker to recall information. Cognitive-lower (or knowledge-recall) test items are easy to write, and as a result it is possible to get too many of them. They can at other times be undervalued and ignored when in fact they are basic and important. For example, the simple item above represents a big shift in knowledge for people who previously may have thought of performance only at the individual and organizational levels. The content validity matrix keeps the number and content location of the cognitive-lower test items in proper proportion.

Taking the same content area, here is a cognitive-higher alternative to the previous question:

First-line supervisors are least responsible for the _____ level of performance.
___X___ A. organizational
_____ B. task
_____ C. process
_____ D. individual

This example of a cognitive-higher item is just over the line from cognitive-lower. It requires recalling information about performance and people responsible for performance. Each could have been a cognitive-lower test item. What makes it cognitive-higher is the judgment required in putting the two knowledge-recall areas together. The other good feature about this item is its consistency with the following criteria:

- The stem is longer than the alternatives.
- The stem should, in clear language, carry the problem statement (the problem statement should not generally be logged in the alternatives).
- There should always be four alternatives for each item.
- Each of the four alternatives should be equally attractive to people not knowing the answer.

Here is a third example, a cognitive-higher item that requires even more complex mental activity:

As a concept, process performance in industry is primarily grounded in _____ theory.

    _____ A. political

    _____ B. economic

    ___X___ C. systems

    _____ D. psychological

Assuming that this item was not directly taught or covered, it requires the interplay of four theories in and the knowledge of process performance versus other forms of performance.

It is worth noting here that HRD is ultimately committed to developing human expertise and improving performance. The criterion-referenced nature of HRD and the organizations in which they function are very different from the norm-referenced perspective on learning that schools have. Unlike schools, gain in knowledge is not the ultimate goal of HRD. Knowledge is one component of expertise (experience is the other), and expertise is one component of performance.

Figures 8.2 and 8.3 show portions of multiple-choice tests.

Developing Matching Test Items The matching item is a modification of the multiple-choice item. Instead of having a stem and alternatives, matching items have a column of premises and a column of responses. Here is an example of a good cognitive-lower matching test item (you should know the answers to it):

Directions: Column A contains a list of subelements of the domains of the Results Assessment System. On the line to the left of each, put the letter from column B that best matches it.

Column A

A	1. Stakeholders
C	2. Financial
B	3. Expertise
A	4. Participants
C	5. System
B	6. Knowledge

Column B

A. Perceptions
B. Learning
C. Performance
D. Results

Use these guidelines in writing matching test items:

- Use homogeneous content material in each item.
- Use short lists with a briefer list of responses to the right.
- Use an uneven numbers of premises and responses (allowing for responses to be used more than once).
- Provide clear and concise directions.

Figure 8.2. Sample Items of a
Total Quality Management Knowledge Test

Name _____

1. *Customer satisfaction* is the sum of:

   a. statistics + inspection + teamwork.

   b. leadership + teamwork + continuous improvement.

   c. continuous improvement + tools + service improvement.

   d. leadership + teamwork.

2. A good *leader* should:

   a. focus primarily on controlling and directing people.

   b. limit the risks the organization takes.

   c. inspire a shared vision of the future.

   d. closely supervise others to see that the work is done right.

3. In order for *brainstorming* to work, which of the following rules must be used?

   a. Each person should work on his or her own ideas.

   b. Limit the number of "wild" ideas.

   c. Don't get too many ideas on the table at once.

   d. Don't make any initial judgment of ideas.

4. The *team leader* is responsible for:

   a. recording the group's ideas.

   b. monitoring how long it takes for the group to accomplish tasks.

   c. doing most of the work between meetings.

   d. observing and monitoring the group process and dynamics.

5. *Flowcharts* are used to:

   a. analyze work processes.

   b. help everyone visualize a process the same way.

   c. identify waste.

   d. all of the above

**Figure 8.2. Sample Items of a
Total Quality Management Knowledge Test, Cont'd.**

6. If a group wants to use a *flowchart*, which of these should be one of the first steps?

    a. Use a problem-solving process to see how the process can be improved.

    b. Obtain data.

    c. Decide on the beginning and ending points for the process to be analyzed.

    d. Eliminate redundant steps.

7. A *fishbone* diagram is also known as a:

    a. Pareto chart.

    b. customer and requirements chart.

    c. checklist.

    d. cause and effect diagram.

8. When conducting a *force field analysis*, one usually draws a line down the center of the page and writes what on either side of the line?

    a. easy and difficult tasks

    b. reasonable and unreasonable goals

    c. helping and hindering forces

    d. good and bad ideas

9. *Checklists* are ideal for:

    a. analyzing problems that might occur in the future.

    b. determining how often an event occurs over a designated period.

    c. displaying data in a meeting.

    d. identifying the causes of an effect.

10. A *histogram* is used to:

    a. show the number of times something happened compared to the number of times other things happened.

    b. show how things change over time.

    c. show the pros and cons of something.

    d. schedule events.

DEVELOPING MEASURES OF RESULTS

Figure 8.3. Sample Items of a Knowledge Test of
Rummler and Brache's *Improving Performance* (1995) Book

—Do Not Write on This Test—

Purpose: Chapter Tests provide a systematic review of the important ideas in each chapter of *Improving Performance*. An *Answer Sheet for Chapter Tests* is provided so that you may check your answers and review text material as needed. Beside each question on the right-hand side of the tests, page numbers are indicated so that you may find the material specifically addressed by each question.

Instructions: Do not write your answers on this test. Write your answers on the separate answer sheet. To check your answers against the correct answers, place the *Chapter Self-Test* on top of the self-tests answer sheet lining up the left-hand side of the *Self-Test* with the corresponding column of answers for the chapter you have completed.

Chapter 1

For answers, see pages in book indicated below.

_____ 1. According to Rummler and Brache, today's business managers _____ performance needs within their organizations.
   A. effectively address   (p. 2)
   B. are unaware
   C. do not understand the variables
   D. expend too much effort improving

_____ 2. A basic issue underlying business concerns such as   (p. 2)
   quality, customer focus, productivity, cycle time, and costs is _____.
   A. entrepreneurship.
   B. organization and individual performance.
   C. training.
   D. employee empowerment.

Chapter 2

_____ 3. A major difference between the "vertical view" and   (pp. 5–9)
   the "systems view" of organizations is _____.
   A. the vertical view is a more comprehensive view.
   B. the vertical view shows the flow of the work.
   C. the systems view does not look outside.
   D. the systems view allows better functional interfaces.

**Figure 8.3. Sample Items of a Knowledge Test of
Rummler and Brache's *Improving Performance* (1995) Book, Cont'd.**

_____ 4. Organizational goals and functional goals are   (pp. 8–9)
most clearly articulated when organizations are
viewed _____.
A. vertically.
B. functionally.
C. as cultures.
D. as systems.

_____ 5. Management emphasis on achieving separate   (pp. 6–7)
departmental goals results in _____.
A. functional optimalization.
B. organizational optimalization.
C. functional suboptimalization.
D. organizational diversification.

_____ 6. "White space" refers to _____.   (p. 9)
A. undocumented management interventions.
B. a component of system flowcharts.
C. the interfaces between boxes on the
organization chart.
D. the unwritten portion of business correspondence.

_____ 7. _____ is the process by which systems   (pp. 12–13)
adjust to environmental changes.
A. Adaptation
B. Retrenchment
C. Diversification
D. Maturation

_____ 8. The key variable in an organization's ability to   (p. 12)
effectively adapt to change is its _____.
A. technology.
B. management.
C. financial status.
D. product line.

Chapter 3

_____ 9. Rummler and Brache's performance improvement   (p. 19)
model is based on the integration of _____
at the *organization, process,* and *job/performer* levels.
A. mission, strategy, and objectives
B. goals, design, and objectives
C. goals, design, and management
D. strategy, structure, and outcomes

**Figure 8.3. Sample Items of a Knowledge Test of
Rummler and Brache's *Improving Performance* (1995) Book, Cont'd.**

_____ 10. The level of performance which addresses business   (p. 15)
strategy, organization structure, and deployment of
resources is _____.
A. the industry level.
B. the organizational level.
C. the process level.
D. the job/performer level.

_____ 11. Work processes are measured _____.   (p. 22)
A. at least quarterly.
B. against last year's performance.
C. to ensure that output is meeting customer needs.
D. to prevent costs from increasing.

_____ 12. Which of the following elements is *not* addressed by   (p. 25)
managers at the *job/performer* level of performance?
A. performance specifications
B. task interference
C. consequences and feedback
D. knowledge and skills
E. shareholder's return on equity

_____ 13. The *organization, process,* and *job/performer* levels   (p. 26)
of performance are _____ in their effects
on performance.
A. interchangeable
B. interdependent
C. independent
D. equivalent

The following matching test item illustrates an item that measures cognitive-higher content of this chapter, and Figure 8.4 shows a portion of the matching items from a personal interaction knowledge test.

Directions: Column A contains a list of actions related to the development and administration of a knowledge test. On the line to the left of each, put the letter from column B that best matches the impact this action has.

Column A

_____C_____ 1. Increase the number of items.

_____B_____ 2. Each participant writes a question for the exam.

_____B_____ 3. Have two students jointly take one test.

_____A_____ 4. Use the task analysis as the basis for the test.

_____D_____ 5. Choose a 10- versus 30-item test.

Column B

A. Raises validity

B. Lowers validity

C. Raises reliability

D. Lowers reliability

Measures of Knowledge in the Sales Communication Case

In the sales communication case, the knowledge of the sales communication aspect of the sales process was organized into five content categories that came from an analysis of the structure of the work. A front-end analysis involving interviews, observations, and records around successful and failed sales efforts served as the source of content. Thus, within the core sales communication process, the knowledge elements and the elements of demonstrating expertise used the same five-part content structure. In another organizational

Figure 8.4. Matching Items on a
Personal Interaction Knowledge Test

Name _____

For each statement in the left column below, select one of the Interactive Skills shown in the right column that *best* describes the statement. Write the letter corresponding to your answer in the Answer block. For example, if you think the first statement is an example of "supporting," write the letter C in the Answer block beside that statement.

Statement	Answer	Interactive Skills
1. Does everyone see what I mean?		**A. Proposing**
2. I suggest we try a new approach.		**B. Building**
3. Let's take your idea a step further and		**C. Supporting**
do that with the whole department.		**D. Disagreeing**
4. Has anything like this been done before?		**E. Defending/ attacking**
5. Chris, what do you think?		**F. Testing understanding**
6. I learned this from another department.		**G. Summarizing**
7. I agree with you.		**H. Seeking information**
8. So far it seems as if we're all agreeing		**I. Giving information**
to try something new.		**J. Shutting out**
9. I just don't think your idea will work.		**K. Bringing in**
10. Thanks for your ideas, Chris, but I think		
we need to move on to other steps.		
11. That's a stupid idea!		

context, the knowledge structure of communication could more closely follow a theory model, with the assessment of communication expertise following a practice structure. Although the two categories of learning in this sales communication case adhere to the same general structure—one is about the knowing part and the other is the doing part—both were deemed important to assess. Thus, from a general planning perspective, the commitment was made to assess both in the initial measurement plan.

The case communication training portion covered the following content areas (note that the product expertise was learned in another training session and is not included here):

Content Areas	Totals	Cognitive-Low	Cognitive-High	Total Items
Openings and closings	30%	10%	20%	15
Value/proof statements	20	5	15	10
Listening	20	10	10	10
Questioning	20	10	10	10
Support materials/visuals	10	10	0	5
Totals	100%	45%	55%	50

A fifty-item instrument of multiple-choice and matching test items was developed and used. Five of the top-performing salespeople took part in the pilot-test session of the course. Their average score was 43. A standard of 40 was established as the standard that participants were required to meet. This test was given toward the end of the training session. Those not getting a score of 40 or higher were allowed to retake the test within two weeks of the completion of the program. In that there was to be a follow-up assessment of expertise back on the job, this built-in opportunity to schedule a retake of the test was included.

DEVELOPING MEASURES OF EXPERTISE

Expertise is defined as human behaviors, acquired through study and experience within a specialized domain, that have effective results and optimal efficiency. Human expertise is the second category of learning in the Results Assessment System.

Most people have an enormous respect for expertise. Those with expertise have knowledge and are able to act on that knowledge. The effective and efficient ability to act comes from experience beyond the base of knowledge.

We generally recommend assessing both knowledge results and expertise results. Measuring expertise, which is done after the learner gains some experience, requires that a person demonstrate behavior in a real or a simulated setting. The amount of experience will vary with the complexity and difficulty of the task. In some instances, limited role-playing and simulation experiences toward the end of a HRD program are enough. At other times, more extensive simulations or supervised fieldwork are required. For example, you may be aware of extended learning experiences built into such jobs as surgeon, nuclear power operator, teacher, and art restorer.

Expertise takes many forms, and those who develop the instrument must have a deep understanding of the expertise to be assessed. Whatever the realm of expertise, however, it can be viewed in terms of end products or processes followed. Like most other issues relating to results assessment, the front-end analysis holds many, if not most, of the critical data to assess expertise.

End-Product Measures

End-product measures assess the qualities of the end product produced by the individual demonstrating expertise. A simple example is the gasser of the pit crew for a Daytona 500 race car. The demonstration of end-product expertise is in getting the gas into the gas tank of the car. From an analysis of the result requirements, it can be determined that getting the gas tank filled in a limited amount of time are the two critical end-product measures.

There are three major steps in developing an end-product measure of expertise within any realm:

1. Determining the primary good or service product (for example, things, events, customers, transaction)
2. Determining the measure of the product measure (for example, quantity, time, quality feature, cost)
3. Establishing a good method of recording product data (one that is reliable and valid)

The information required for steps 1 and 2 can be taken directly from task analysis documentation (structure and documentation of the work or the subject matter). And usually there already is a data recording method in place in the organization for step 3. For example, we found in the sales communication case that the company already carefully defined and tracked sales by product, region, manager, and individual salesperson. Another client, a manufacturer that produced plastic pipe, had a very good data collection system in place that continuously assessed and recorded the type and quantity of pipe produced, as well as the quality features of all product produced. If no measure is available, however, the information from steps 1 and 2 will need to be converted into a practical data collection instrument.

Process Measures

Process measures assess the rigorous adherence to the required process steps and procedures exhibited by the person demonstrating expertise. Look at the simple example of the gasser of the pit crew for a Daytona 500 race car. The demonstration of process expertise is adhering to the procedures and principles required for getting the gas in the gas tank of the race car. From an analysis of the results requirements, it can be determined that following the procedural steps in filling the gas tank and adhering to the two safety principles are the two critical process measures.

There are four major steps in developing a process measure of expertise within any realm:

1. Determining the primary good or service product (for example, things, events, customers, transaction)
2. Determining the procedures required of the process
3. Determining the principles that undergird the process
4. Establishing an observational check sheet of the procedures and principles (reliable and valid)

The information required for steps 1, 2, and 3 can be taken directly from task analyses. Often this information can almost be reformatted and turned into the final check sheet, which is step 4. For example, a twenty-step procedure for a pilot flight check process could become the assessment rating sheet. A more complex example would be if you wanted division managers to manage for creativity as part of their job. It you work in an organization that provides financial services to large numbers of individual clients, there is a great deal of opportunity to innovate and improve in ways that will increase investment assets.

An analysis of the corporate creativity process yielded six principles or elements of creativity: alignment, self-initiated activity, unofficial activity, serendipity, diverse stimuli, and within-company communication (Robinson and Stern, 1997). These principles, along with their subelements, could be converted into a rating sheet that would require the rater either to (1) assess whether there is any evidence of its existence or (2) rate the degree of evidence (none, low, medium, or high) in the light of a description of the degree levels.

Sometimes you are interested in assessing just product or process, and sometimes a blend of both.

Sales Communication Case Expertise Assessment

In this case, the sales communication expertise was organized into content categories that matched the flow of expert work behavior. (As already noted, the knowledge elements and the elements of demonstrating expertise used the same content structure. Many times they are different.)

The content areas for the sales communication training portion were the basis of the measure of knowledge and expertise. Sales managers served as expert raters and rated the learners in a high-fidelity sales simulation that culminated the training event. They were trained to discern specific differences between the "above, meets, and below" ratings. The same managers finally rated each of the learners in an actual sales situation back on the job within sixty days of the training portion of this total improvement effort using the following instrument:

	Rating Against Standard		
Content Areas	1 point Below	2 points Meets	3 points Above
• Openings and closings	_____	_____	_____
• Value/proof statements	_____	_____	_____
• Listening	_____	_____	_____
• Questioning	_____	_____	_____
• Support materials/visuals	_____	_____	_____
Totals	_____	_____	_____
Total Points	_____	_____	_____

The goal was for each learner to obtain a "meets the standard" score at the completion of the training. Using the 1–3 scale, this would mean that each participant was to demonstrate expertise at an average of 2.0 or higher.

The raters had more specific details for each of the six elements of the sales process listed above and the learners also had been trained in those subcomponents. For example, the "opening and closing" had three major subcomponents: (1) got attention, (2) used an overview statement within two minutes, and (3) established a clear call to action resulting in the next step in the sales process.

Figures 8.5 and 8.6 are examples of measures of expertise.

STATISTICAL ANALYSIS OF TEST DATA

There are several basic statistical analyses that can be run on tests and test items to confirm and improve test validity and reliability. Our first concern is that you build in reliability and validity.

The information technology is changing rapidly and makes the job easier. Two important developments relate to how data are entered into computer databases and the availability of simple soft-ware designed to analyze test data (Swanson and Mattson, 1998). In terms of data entry, learners increasingly have the opportunity to respond by computer, and low-cost data scanners for test answer sheets are available. These scanners can score tests immediately and enter the raw data into a database.

Given such technological support, here are several statistical analyses you could perform:

- Test reliability. The KR 21 reliability test informs you of the consistency of the measure (a correlation coefficient from .65 and up is good; commercially available measures should have .85 reliability or higher).
- Test concurrent validity. The correlation of the test data with a second measure of the same content confirms the validity of the

Figure 8.5. Sample Items of a Sales Communication Expertise Test

Name: Date:

0 **Unable to Observe** No opportunity to observe.	1 **Not evident** Does not demonstrate.	2 **Functional** Applies skills: requires some guidance.	3 **Proficient** Uses skills in complex situations. Minimal guidance.	4 **Expert** Coaches and supports others.

	Job Specific Tasks Ratings →	0	1	2	3	4
1.	Communicate during the presale subprocess.					
2.	Reconcile disjoints between customer expectations and company capabilities.					
3.	Partner with Implementation Manager to complete implementation.					
4.	Finalize financial contracts and manage performance guarantees.					
5.	Case Setup: Implement and maintain banking procedure, structure claim reporting, and provide case experience.					
6.	Monitor enrollment and re-enrollment process.					
7.	Contact customer proactively and communicate network and product developments.					
8.	Develop and execute integral renewal strategy.					
9.	Sell additional business to existing client.					
10.	Negotiate, prepare, and deliver settlement package including reports.					
11.	Manage canceled coverage.					

For any rating of two (2) or lower, please attach the specific task page with explanations.

Copies to: 1. Sales Manager 2. Sales Performance Consulting 3. Employee

**Figure 8.5. Sample Items of a Sales
Communication Expertise Test, Cont'd.**

Name: Date:

0 Unable to Observe No opportunity to observe.	1 Not evident Does not demonstrate.	2 Functional Applies skills: requires some guidance.	3 Proficient Uses skills in complex situations. Minimal guidance.	4 Expert Coaches and supports others.

	Job Specific Tasks Ratings →	0	1	2	3	4
1.	Create, execute, and constantly improve local market strategy and tactics to achieve plan.					
2.	Create an environment that drives results.					
3.	Manage and improve the sales and account management process.					
4.	Select, build, and coach individuals on the sales team.					
5.	Drive prospect activity and establish presence with producers and business community.					
6.	Build productive internal relationships with matrix partners.					

For any rating of two (2) or lower, please attach the specific task page with explanations.

Copies to: 1. Sales Manager 2. Sales Performance Consulting 3. Employee

Figure 8.6. Sample Task Rating Worksheet for Sales Manager Task

Name:	Date:	Overall Rating:

Sales Mgr. Task 4	Select, build, and coach individuals on the sales and account management team.
Overall Performance **Result**	• Sales staff members meet standards identified for their respective positions. • Sales and client management/existing business account executive staff meet quotas as identified in the Compensation Manual.

0 Unable to Observe No opportunity to observe.	1 Not evident Does not demonstrate.	2 Functional Applies skills: requires some guidance.	3 Proficient Uses skills in complex situations. Minimal guidance.	4 Expert Coaches and supports others.

If your overall rating is two or less, please rate
the components below individually:

Knowledge—Must Know	Rate #	Expertise—Must Do	Rate #
• What organizational, process, and individual variables are impacting individual performance.		• Take responsibility for coaching and training.	
• Company's human resource policies, procedures and performance management process.		• Train, coach, and assess sales staff to ensure they are "experts" on company products, medical management capabilities, service, and Health Plan operations.	

**Figure 8.6. Sample Task Rating
Worksheet for Sales Manager Task, Cont'd.**

• Behavioral interviewing techniques and how to use and apply competency profiles.		• Train, coach, and assess sales staff to ensure they can effectively communicate company's competitive advantage.	
• Staff members' backgrounds, strengths, weaknesses, and development interests.		• Train and coach sales staff on how company makes money: how to use various tools to convey company's advantage.	
• Roles, responsibilities, and objectives of each position.		• Train sales staff on financial model (contracting, capitation, etc.)	
• Products, prospect/client needs/expectations, key decision makers, their backgrounds, and goals.		• Hire highly motivated, highly skilled people	
• How to develop the organizational skills of a sales staff.		• Develop and communicate clear performance expectations	
		• Work to eliminate organization and process roadblocks which prevent individuals from performing their jobs.	
		• Ensure that sales staff know each sales/account management process step well and how to progress from one step to the next as needed.	

**Figure 8.6. Sample Task Rating
Worksheet for Sales Manager Task, Cont'd.**

		• Meet with sales staff regularly to review quantity and quality of activity.	
		• Develop people to be independent success stories.	
		• Exhibit patience with progressive development.	
		• Lead reports to conduct honest self-appraisal.	
		• Recognize and celebrate success and extraordinary effort.	
		• Set up and follow through on field-based new-hire training process.	
		• Maximize use of Sales Performance Consulting's programs (e.g. Advanced Sales School).	
		• Conduct group training sessions (case review; general coaching; and "stump speech").	
		• Use guest speakers (e.g. senior staff) to emphasize points in training sessions.	
		• Role plays with staff.	

test (+ 1.00 correlation is perfect positive and 1.00 correlation is perfect negative; .00 correlation is no relationship).

- Test item difficulty. The percentage of those who answered an item correctly (and an average percentage correct of all the test items for overall test difficulty) informs you of the item difficulty (e.g., 60 percent correct, 82 percent correct).

- Test item discrimination. A comparison of the number of people in the upper half of the total test scores and the lower half who answered the item correctly. More people in the upper half should get any one item correct.

CONCLUSION

The HRD profession can almost single-handedly deliver learning results in the form of essential knowledge and expertise. In this age of knowledge work, with rapidly changing requirements for expertise, assessing and reporting learning results are essential to reaching and confirming this contribution to organizations and individuals who work in them.

KEY POINTS TO REMEMBER

▼

- Good measures are reliable and valid.
- Use a content validity matrix to build in content validity.
- Use larger numbers of items or observations to build in reliability.
- Use multiple-choice or matching items for tests of knowledge.
- Use product measures or process measures for tests of expertise.

CHAPTER

9

Perception Results

Measuring Participant
and Stakeholder Outcomes

Assessment Problem: How do I create or select good measures of perceptions? More specifically, how do I select or develop measures of participant and stakeholder perception results?

▼

A perception is a personal feeling, impression, belief, or comprehension of an object, event, or quality that may or may not be factual. Within the Results Assessment System, results of the status or changes in perceptions are classified into two categories:

Participant perceptions: Perceptions of people having firsthand
  experience with systems, processes, people, goods, or services.
Stakeholder perceptions: Perceptions of leaders of systems and people having a vested interest in the desired results and the means
  of achieving them.

Perceptions of performance and learning outcomes are not good measures of actual performance and learning outcomes. Nevertheless, organizations are susceptible to the power of human perceptions, accurate or inaccurate, even when there are more credible measures of performance and learning available. Thus, the concern for participant and stakeholder perceptions cannot be ignored, even though perceptions may be less important when it comes to assessing facts. Organizational leaders and HRD professionals should be able to assess human perceptions and any changes in them correctly and interpret their impact as part of an overall results profile. When you are able to measure and present positive results—"the consequence of a particular action, operation or course" (*American Heritage*, 1993, p. 1164)—you increase the odds of obtaining and continuing to obtain additional support from everyone at every level.

THE LIMITATIONS OF PERCEPTIONS

Perceptions are in the minds of the beholders. The limited and tricky side of a perception is that the individual can strongly believe in it, yet it can be wrong. Suppose your product is truly the best in the marketplace, but customers falsely perceive that another product is best. This is a big problem for you and the customers because both end up losing. In the absence of facts, perceptions rule. One purpose of products like *Consumer Reports* and the Results Assessment System is to counter false perceptions with facts. They establish practical and credible measures of a service or product, provide tests, and report the test results. In contrast, marketers often counter false perceptions with their own perceptions of the truth, not necessarily perceptions based on external facts.

We are reminded of the story of when Lee Iaccoca became the president of Chrysler Corporation. The facts clearly showed that Dodge trucks were as durable as the competition's, but potential customers perceived them to be less durable. When Iaccoca delved into the perceptions of potential truck buyers, he discovered that they had very positive feelings about the ram's head (which had been the Dodge symbol), and they perceived older Dodge vehicles as more durable than the new models.

Iaccoca reincarnated the ram symbol—the Dodge Ram—and placed a ram hood ornament on each Dodge truck. He also started a television advertisement campaign, talking to viewers about tough Dodge trucks. As he was speaking, an actual Dodge truck was dropped behind him from above. It crashed to the ground unharmed, whereupon Iaccoca touted its toughness. In a short time, Dodge trucks sales rose significantly, presumably as a result of customers' perception that Dodge trucks were much more durable than they previously believed. As for the trucks themselves, they were the same trucks before and after. The actual high durability—something apart from customer perception—had not changed.

Sometimes you need to consider carefully the facts outside the person and the perceptions within the person in order to get the total picture. For example, it is our understanding that Chrysler Corporation also decided that improving the durability of its trucks (characteristics inherent in the truck itself, which are outside people's perceptions) would sustain the growing perception that Dodge trucks were durable.

Perceptions have important value, but they have limitations as well. Imagine if the perceptions about various trucks and their features were obtained from people who were never going to buy a truck under any condition. The core limitation is that what people feel or believe—their perceptions—and what they do—their individual performance—can be totally disconnected.

Because perceptions are powerful and easily distorted or misinterpreted, it is important to pursue them with clarity. If the core results being assessed are logically outside the perceptions of individuals, then that is where the results assessment should be focused. For example, if you want an assessment of air quality, you should use a direct performance measure of actual air quality, not perceptions of it. If you want to know if an organization performed better as a result of an intervention, do not ask for people's perceptions of performance change; instead obtain direct measures of performance before and after the intervention.

It is important to think through the limitations of perceptions to prevent collecting invalid data and basing decisions on such data. However, the correct location of the desired data can be either perceptions inside the person or appropriate facts outside the person, depending on your measurement objectives. For example, why ask somebody how old she thinks a building is that she never owned when the city has official deeds and records as to its age? On the other hand, to ask people if they like the building or are comfortable in it is perfectly appropriate.

Perception in a time frame of the present or future is also important. This is illustrated by the familiar reports we hear about election polls. When reporting perceptions gained from potential voters, analysts are rightfully cautious about the data. They are always careful to note that they are reporting their estimate of the election outcome "if the election was held today." Analysts also have to estimate if the people they obtained perception data from will actually turn out to vote in the future. All of this attitudinal reaction makes for great speculation and conversation but has very little utility in getting to the facts of the situation.

WHAT PERCEPTIONS SHOULD BE ASSESSED

There are two fundamental foci of perception assessments, processes and outcomes, each with unique issues and considerations.

Process Perceptions

Process perceptions are defined as perceptions about ongoing processes, including the intervention process itself. They are most commonly collected from participants (employees, customers, and others), although it may make sense to collect them from stakeholders (such as managers, shareholders, and citizens) as well. The primary purpose of process perceptions is to understand how people react to the quality features of the process. Examples might include perceptions of the integrity of a work process, feedback following a team-building session, or periodic surveys during implementation of a quality program.

Process perceptions can be thought of further in terms of affect and utility (Alliger, Tannenbaum, Bennett, Traver, and Shotland, 1997; Warr and Bunce, 1995). Affective perceptions are typically concerned with enjoyment and satisfaction with the intervention. Surveys in this group often include items relating to enjoyment of activities, facilities, materials, and other such factors. Because participants are often viewed as customers, these factors cannot be ignored. However, in the case of HRD, research has consistently found that affective perceptions have very little or no correlation to learning or follow-up performance.

For this reason we recommend using the average score or division between the positive and negative as a minimum standard for affective perceptions (for example, 2.5 on a four-point rating scale). The

Enter-Train-Ment

The false notion that participants should have positive reactions to training sessions and instructors has negatively affected the HRD profession. Almost every training session in the United States asks participant to react to their training experience. The familiar "smile sheet" almost always focuses on the secondary variables, such as if the instructor "kept the session alive and interesting" and participants' reaction to the "comfort and convenience" of the facilities. In contrast to these perceptions about secondary aspects, assessment of the most important results from training, learning, and performance, is seldom done. Thus, enormous pressure is placed on planners and presenters to get high participant ratings from the event and to treat the actual learning among participants as secondary. Traditional training talks about the other levels of evaluation while providing the false idea that high participant ratings are a proxy for high learning. They are not (Dixon, 1990). Sadly, trainers hardly ever get beyond participant reactions. The spin-off from this inaccurate view of evaluation is an entire industry of consultants and publications focused on "fun-filled training" to help trainers get their ratings up. Davis and Davis (1998) call this "enter-trainment" and chide the profession for letting this approach get in the way of effective training strategies—strategies that result in actual learning, not high necessarily participant reactions.

Here are two quick examples of this misuse of participant reaction assessment from our own experience. One is from a large oil company and the other from a major financial organization.

The personnel development department in the oil company used us to deliver training sessions in three-day programs that were offered four times a year. In the ten years of our participation, the only evaluation used was participant reactions (attitudinal reactions) of how the participants perceived the training program using superficial questions on a 1–10 point scale (with 10 being the highest). Any presenter getting less than a 9 rating more than once was let go. After ten years, we were the only consultant-presenters left from the original list. Getting results in the form of high participant ratings is not hard. But were these the important results for such a high-level development effort?

The financial corporation brought us in to audit the effectiveness of its executive development programs. We found out that the one standout program in the eyes of the participants had no evidence of impact on corporate performance. This was after eight years of offering this popular program to every top manager in the corporation—hundreds of people. All of the other fourteen programs produced evidence of corporate change and improved performance. If the desired result is learning, the measure should be one of the actual knowledge or expertise, not participant perceptions of the instructor, the room, or even their own learning. We recommended that the highly rated program be eliminated.

best HRD interventions are confusing at times and hard work for the participants. Ratings that are too high may indicate "enter-train-ment"; ratings that are too low may indicate poor customer service. The aim is find a midrange where participants are happy enough, but not to focus extensively on affective measures.

Utility perceptions, on the other hand, are proving to be more robust. Utility questions inquire about the perceived usefulness or applicability of what has been learned in the intervention. Usually they include questions about how useful the new tool will be on the job, whether it was applicable, or how much support will be given for its use.

Research indicates that utility data are more highly correlated with performance and learning outcomes than affect data, though still not at high levels. The difference is substantial enough that we recommend that you emphasize collecting utility perceptions, that is, if perception data are to be used at all. The logic is simple: if you are going to collect perceptions, at least ask for perceptions of the core variables related to performance and learning.

Outcome Perceptions

Outcome perceptions are quite similar to utility perceptions concerning processes, except that they ask individuals their perceptions of actual outcomes, not expected ones. Outcome perceptions are the more important ones to collect from stakeholders, because it is the outcomes in the form of performance that they are usually seeking. Participants are also frequently asked to report on their perceptions of outcomes associated with an HRD intervention.

In most cases valid measures of the desired performance are factually based, not perceptually based. Thus, perceptions of outcomes serve as indicator measures (for example, "87 percent of the respondents believe their job performance improved due to the team building") rather than actual performance measures. In most situations, the assessor can choose between directly collecting performance data (preferred) and collecting indicator data in the form of perceptions.

One commonly used form of performance indicator measure is supervisor ratings of performance change after a development effort. When it is impractical or politically difficult to collect actual performance data, perceptions of outcomes become the best possible alternative measure. And there are instances when participant and stakeholder perceptions of outcomes are the appropriate outcome measure: when the outcome of interest is internal or personal. For example, if the desired outcome of an intervention is to improve job attitudes, then clearly the only way to assess the outcome is to ask employees about their attitudes. Another example is organizational climate or culture change. Typically the outcomes of interest are employee perceptions of the culture or climate, although other views can be used as well. Because employee behavior is shaped by their perceptions of the organization, regardless of whether the perception is "real," it is quite appropriate to collect perception measures for climate and culture. If an intervention is focused on culture change, then perceptions may be an appropriate measure of the intervention results.

HOW TO BUILD VALID AND RELIABLE MEASURES OF PERCEPTIONS

The issues related to building good measures of perceptions are the same as for performance and learning: validity and reliability. Content validity is logical, not statistical. Since soliciting perceptions of people is a common practice and has appearances of being relatively easy, we have found that producing a measure of perceptions in the form of a questionnaire or survey instrument can easily get out of hand. People often begin the process by asking, "Wouldn't it be interesting to find out what people think about this or that?" Before you know it, the perception instrument is a hodgepodge of interesting but disconnected questions with no logical base.

Content Validity

The content validity of a measure of perception is critical. Because this may be the biggest problem in developing measures of perceptions, we offer two bits of advice:

- Measure the right domain.
- Use a sound content model as the template.

In measuring the right domain, it is important to ask, "Where are the facts?" When the facts are outside the perceptions of people, go to the source of the facts; do not ask people what they *think* the facts are. For example, assessing the perception of people as to whether they think they learned is very different from assessing their actual learning. You might care about what people both actually learned and perceived to have learned, and it is okay to measure both, as long as you do not confuse the interpretation of the results from these two domains.

As for using a content model as a template, this is similar to the content validity matrix discussed in Chapter Eight. For example, the Baldrige Quality Award criteria provide an established template of the seven elements of quality: Leadership, Information and Analysis, Strategic Quality Planning, Human Resource Utilization, Quality Assurance of Products and Services, Quality Results, and Customer Satisfaction. We used these criteria as the basis of the content validity of an instrument—perception dimensions and specific items—to assess the statewide perception of the effort expended by Minnesota Businesses and Industries and attainment of the quality components. The perception instrument we used, shown as Figure 9.1, displays the core Baldrige criteria and the two scales used to obtain the perceptions of business leaders.

Development of Items

There are three basic concerns in developing items for a measure of perception. They may sound like common sense, but as the saying goes, "There is nothing common about common sense." Take the time to apply these three guidelines:

1. Simplicity. Do not try to assess more than a single point in each item.
2. Wording. Use short sentences or descriptors, common words, the same tense, and no double negatives.
3. Scales. When using a Likert scale, use either a four-point or five-point scale; also assign value meanings to the numbers, such as (4) excellent, (3) good, (2) poor, and (1) unacceptable.

Figure 9.1. Sample Perception Instrument: Minnesota Quality Improvement Practices Survey

Survey Code Number _____

ANNUAL CENSUS BY THE UNIVERSITY OF MINNESOTA AND THE MINNESOTA COUNCIL FOR QUALITY

Purpose of the Survey:

This survey is to establish a scientifically accurate profile of quality improvement practices in Minnesota business and industry having 50 or more employees. The questions are based on the Malcolm Baldrige National Quality Award examination categories.

Anonymity:

All responses to this survey will remain anonymous. Your survey code number is all we need to see that your data are put in the appropriate business/industry group. We will be personally contacting non-respondents to ensure a 100% return, and that is why we initially need to have the surveys coded.

Definitions:

- *Quality*—a reliable product or service that meets or exceeds customer requirements at a price that they are willing to pay.
- *Quality Improvement*—a systematic approach used to reduce variations in the processes which produce a product or service.
- *Informal Quality Improvement Effort*—an encouraged and expected outcome without direct involvement and leadership from senior management and financial commitment.
- *Formal Quality Improvement Effort*—a defined plan of cultural change and process study including senior management leadership and training of employees in problem-solving statistics.

Part A—*Background Data* (Please *circle* the correct responses)

Yes No 1. Are you the person whose name appears on the cover letter?
(If no, please identify yourself by name and job title _____.)

Yes No 2. Does your organization have a *formal* quality improvement effort? (If yes, is there __ Designated leadership? __ Financial commitment? __ Training? __ Regular reporting?)

19___ 3. What year did you establish a formal quality effort?

Yes No 4. Is there a person in your firm who is credited with being the *first* champion of the quality effort in your firm? (If yes, what was his/her job title? _____ Was he/she considered: __ Top management; __ Middle management; __ Worker)

Figure 9.1. Sample Perception Instrument: Minnesota Quality Improvement Practices Survey, Cont'd.

Yes   No   5. Is there a person in your firm who is *now* credited with being the champion of the quality effort in your firm? (If yes, what is his/her job
title? _____ Was he/she considered: ___ Top management; ___ Middle management; ___ Worker)

Yes   No   6. Does your firm develop and retain systematic documentation of your quality improvement effort? (If Yes, are you willing to share this with
case study researchers? Yes – No)

Yes   No   7. Was there a critical event associated with the origin of your quality improvement effort? (If yes, describe: _____

_____

Part B—Quality Improvement Practices (based on the Malcolm Baldrige Award)

1.0   Leadership (senior executives create and sustain clear and visible quality value and quality management systems).

Effort Level low–med–high	Items within Leadership category	Status level Awareness	Planning	Action	Attainment
L M H	1.1 Senior Executive Leadership	_____	_____	_____	_____
L M H	1.2 Quality Values	_____	_____	_____	_____
L M H	1.3 Management for Quality	_____	_____	_____	_____
L M H	1.4 Public Responsibility	_____	_____	_____	_____
L M H	*Overall assessment of 1.0 Leadership category practices*	_____	_____	_____	_____

Comments: _____

2.0 Information and Analysis (purposeful data collection and data utilization underlying the quality improvement effort).

Effort Level low-med-high	Items within Info. & Analysis category	Status level Awareness	Planning	Action	Attainment
L M H	2.1 Scope & Management of Quality Data and Information	___	___	___	___
L M H	2.2 Analysis of Quality Data and Information	___	___	___	___
L M H	Overall assessment of 2.0 Information and Analysis category practices	___	___	___	___

Comments:

3.0 Strategic Quality Planning (integrates quality improvement into overall business planning).

Effort Level low-med-high	Items within Strat. Quality Plan category	Status level Awareness	Planning	Action	Attainment
L M H	3.1 Strategic Quality Planning Process	___	___	___	___
L M H	3.2 Quality Leadership Indicators in Planning	___	___	___	___
L M H	3.3 Quality Priorities	___	___	___	___
L M H	Overall assessment of 3.0 Strategic Quality Planning category practices	___	___	___	___

Comments:

Figure 9.1. Sample Perception Instrument: Minnesota Quality Improvement Practices Survey, Cont'd.

4.0 Human Resource Utilization (develop and realize the full potential of the workforce).

Effort Level low-med-high	Items *within Human Resource Util. category*	Status level Awareness	Planning	Action	Attainment
L M H	4.1 Human Resource Management	___	___	___	___
L M H	4.2 Employee Involvement	___	___	___	___
L M H	4.3 Quality Education &Training	___	___	___	___
L M H	4.4 Employee Recogntion & Perf. Measurement	___	___	___	___
L M H	4.5 Employee Well-Being & Morale	___	___	___	___
L M H	*Overall assessment of 4.0 Human Resource Utilization category practices*	___	___	___	___

Comments:

5.0 Quality Assurance of Products and Services (systematic approach for total quality control of goods and services).

Effort Level low-med-high	Items *within Quality Assurance of P&S category*	Status level Awareness	Planning	Action	Attainment
L M H	5.1 Design & Introduction of Quality Products & Services	___	___	___	___
L M H	5.2 Process & Quality Control	___	___	___	___
L M H	5.3 Continuous Improvement of Processes, Products, & Services	___	___	___	___
L M H	5.4 Quality Assessment	___	___	___	___
L M H	5.5 Documentation	___	___	___	___
L M H	5.6 Quality Assurance/Assessment & Quality Improvement of Support Service & Business Processes	___	___	___	___
L M H	5.7 Quality Assurance/Assessment & Quality Improvement of Suppliers	___	___	___	___
L M H	*Overall assessment of 5.0 Quality Assurance of Products and Services category*	___	___	___	___

Comments:

6.0 Quality Results (objective measures of meeting customer requirements and comparisons to competing firms).

Effort Level low-med-high	Items within Quality Results category	Status level Awareness	Planning	Action	Attainment
L M H	6.1 Quality of Products and Services	——	——	——	——
L M H	6.2 Comparison of Quality Results	——	——	——	——
L M H	6.3 Business Process, Operational Support Service Quality Improvement	——	——	——	——
L M H	6.4 Supplier Quality Improvement	——	——	——	——
L M H	Overall assessment of 6.0 Quality Results category	——	——	——	——

Comments:

7.0 Customer Satisfaction (knowledge of the customer and systems for customer service).

Effort Level low-med-high	Items within Customer Satisfaction category	Status level Awareness	Planning	Action	Attainment
L M H	7.1 Knowledge of Customer Requirements & Expectations	——	——	——	——
L M H	7.2 Customer Relationship Management	——	——	——	——
L M H	7.3 Customer Service Standards	——	——	——	——
L M H	7.4 Commitment to Customers	——	——	——	——
L M H	7.5 Complaint Resolution for Quality Improvement	——	——	——	——
L M H	7.6 Customer Satisfaction Results	——	——	——	——
L M H	7.7 Customer Satisfaction Comparison	——	——	——	——
L M H	Overall assessment of 7.0 Customer Satisfaction category	——	——	——	——

Comments:

Figure 9.1. Sample Perception Instrument: Minnesota Quality Improvement Practices Survey, Cont'd.

Part C—Product and Service Development in Relation to Quality Improvement

1. What percent of your sales do you think are generated from products and/or services developed over the past three years? _____ %

2. Would you say your firm is (1) more active, (2) less active, or (3) about the same in terms of its efforts in developing new products and services as compared to three years ago? _____.

Part D—Summary Questions

Effort Level	Status level	Awareness	Planning	Action	Attainment
low-med-high					
L M H	Overall assessment of Quality Results	____	____	____	____
L M H	Overall assessment of Leadership Practices	____	____	____	____

THANK YOU!
We will send you a copy of the survey results. Please feel free to contact us if you have questions.

MINNESOTA QUALITY IMPROVEMENT SURVEY
Human Resource Development Research Center
University of Minnesota, 1954 Buford Avenue
St. Paul, MN 55108

DEVELOPING MEASURES
OF PARTICIPANT PERCEPTIONS

Participant perceptions are gathered from people having firsthand experience with systems, processes, people, goods, or services. This experience allows them to speak with authority, so it is important that the scope of the questions and the realm of experience match.

The most fundamental quality about measuring participant perceptions is to make sure that those getting the instrument actually experienced the phenomena. It would be foolish for a business to ask people how well they liked their services if they had never experienced the company's service or to ask the supervisor of a trainee if the instructor did a good job presenting the course content. In this example, both parties can be asked questions, but the questions must draw on the limits of their experience.

In the sales communication case, the participants' perceptions related to the training portion of the improvement effort were assessed. The measure was unique compared to traditional trainee reaction forms of affect. Its content focused on participant utility perceptions of self rather than external factors (such as the instructor or classroom). Holton's (1996) training transfer model was used as the basis of content validity. His five predictors of transfer are ability, motivation to learn, motivation to transfer, expected utility, and link to organizational goals. These variables were turned into the items shown in Figure 9.2 on a measure of participant perceptions related to the participants' learning experience. The data from the five perception items were quite useful. The responsibility for learning was partially shifted from the instructor to the participant, and the data helped identify individuals and work settings requiring additional support to ensure the ultimate use of the learning.

Figure 9.2. Trainee-Participant Perception Form

Program Title _____ Date _____

Presenter(s) _____

Please answer the following questions to help us improve future programs.

	High	Moderate	Some	Low
1. My ability in the content area of this program.	____	____	____	____
2. My level of knowledge/ expertise in this area prior to the program.	____	____	____	____
3. My motivation to learn this new material.	____	____	____	____
4. My supervisor's encourage- ment in learning this new material.	____	____	____	____
5. The expectation that I will use part of this program?	____	____	____	____

What was the most valuable part of this program for you?_____

_____

_____

What was the least valuable part of this program for you?_____

_____

_____

Additional comments would be appreciated. _____

_____

_____

_____

Participant Name (optional)

DEVELOPING MEASURES
OF STAKEHOLDER PERCEPTIONS

Stakeholder perceptions are the perceptions of leaders of systems or people having a vested interest in the desired results and the means of achieving them. These stakeholders can be inside or outside the organization, or producers or consumers, or have a primary or secondary authority and investment in the system under scrutiny.

Liquid Carbonic Corporation decided as part of a companywide quality and performance improvement effort to create an employee newsletter that highlighted the organization's goals, the programs of work, and employee contributions at all levels. Part of the work was to survey the perceptions of the employees as to the effectiveness of the newsletter. Figure 9.3 is the perception instrument that the organization used. A similar measure could go to corporate shareholders or community members.

A related example is AMSCO, a manufacturer of door and window screens, committed to implementing its strategic plans (Sleezer and Swanson, 1992). The change process required that employees at all levels develop a new level of trust and participation. The twenty organizational culture factors identified by McLean (1988) were held up against AMSCO's strategic plan. Six of the culture factors were determined to be directly tied to the plan:

- Job evaluation/job satisfaction
- Work efficiency
- Training and development
- Communication
- Management effectiveness
- View of the organization

**Figure 9.3. Instrument to Measure Employee
Perceptions of the Company Newsletter**

LIQUID NEWS SURVEY—a survey of employees' opinions
about Liquid News

INSTRUCTIONS: Please use a No. 2 pencil
to *fill in* the circles [●] that match your opinions.
Use the back to write comments in your own words.
Please return before May 1st.

Basic Information: *Choose one (1) in each category*

---

1. Job Role: Manager/Supervisor   Non-manager/Non-supervisor

2. Years at Liquid: ○ 0–1   ○ 1–5   ○ 6–19   ○ 20+

3. Functional role:

    ○ Sales/Marketing   ○ Customer Service   ○ Finance/Accounting
    ○ Production   ○ Administration   ○ Information Systems
    ○ Technical   ○ Distribution   ○ General Management

4. Business Unit:

    ○ Carbon Dioxide   ○ Bulk Gas Products   ○ Cylinder Gas Products
    ○ Freezing Systems ○ International   ○ Process Plants
    ○ Industries   ○ LNG, Supercritical, Non-cryogenic Systems

Your Evaluation of Liquid News: *Please answer all questions!*

---

5. Have you been receiving copies of Liquid News?   Yes   No
                                                     ○   ○

6. Are you satisfied with the Liquid News goal?   Yes   No
    "To inform you about the people, businesses,   ○   ○
    and events occurring at Liquid Carbonic"

**Figure 9.3. Instrument to Measure Employee
Perceptions of the Company Newsletter, Cont'd.**

Sections of Liquid News		Always	Sometimes	Never
Do you read them? If read, are you satisfied? (Always-Sometimes-Never)				
		A	S	N
7. President's Message	Read	O	O	O
	Satisfied	O	O	O
		A	S	N
8. Focus on general business news	Read	O	O	O
	Satisfied	O	O	O
		A	S	N
9. Focus on business development	Read	O	O	O
	Satisfied	O	O	O
		A	S	N
10. Focus on international	Read	O	O	O
	Satisfied	O	O	O
		A	S	N
11. Quality & Safety	Read	O	O	O
	Satisfied	O	O	O
		A	S	N
12. Close-ups on Liquid People	Read	O	O	O
	Satisfied	O	O	O
		A	S	N
13. Liquid's Past	Read	O	O	O
	Satisfied	O	O	O
		A	S	N
14. Promotions-Appointments-	Read	O	O	O
Service Anniversaries	Satisfied	O	O	O

Overall Assessment *(items 15–16 and your written comments on the back):*

	Always	Sometimes	Never
15. Liquid News is achieving its stated goal.	A	S	N
	O	O	O
16. I am satisfied with Liquid News.	A	S	N
	O	O	O

**Figure 9.3. Instrument to Measure Employee
Perceptions of the Company Newsletter, Cont'd.**

Provide us comments in your own words
(Please do not *write outside the boxes)*.

17. What do you like best about Liquid News?

18. How do you think Liquid News could be improved?

A preaddressed and stamped envelope is enclosed.
Please mail your completed survey to:

Data Service
Ridge Drive
St. Paul, Minnesota 55101

The pools of items from McLean's lists for each of these factors served as the source of perception items. Ten items for each of the six culture factors were selected to produce a sixty-item measure of AMSCO employee perceptions that was administered before, during, and after the intervention. The measure is shown in Figure 9.4. This instrument was critical in assessing the perception results along a three-year time line, and it proved invaluable in overcoming the emotional and random perceptions that were present in the company. Another noteworthy point is that every employee received summary reports of the data, had easy access to the full reports, and attended small group discussion sessions following each report so as to clarify meaning and plan actions.

In the sales communication case, the regional sales managers held a pivotal role in the process of getting improved sales results. The improvement effort was being directed from the corporate level, but without initial and continuing support of the regional sales managers, the effort would likely falter and perhaps die. At various stages, each sales manager's perception of a major phase of the project was sought. For example, the e-mail survey in Figure 9.5, asking two simple questions and one open-ended question, was sent to each manager.

It was determined that the first two questions would elicit all the core information needed to make sure the effort was on track, and that anything unexpected would show up in the third question.

Managers also appreciated this short instrument (instruments like this commonly get bloated beyond their purpose) and the fact they were not asked to speculate on matters they had not directly experienced. We recommend that these three questions be sent to every supervisor of every trainee of every training program to obtain stakeholder perceptions of the value of each program.

Figure 9.4. Employee Survey of Organizational Culture

AMSCO CORPORATE CULTURE SURVEY

YOUR JOB CATEGORY (check one)

Salaried Exempt	Hourly Production
☐ Engineer	☐ Mills (mills, preassembly)
☐ Manufacturing	☐ Finals (framepress, finals)
☐ Material Management	☐ Doors
(acctg. personnel, gen. admin.)	☐ Combos
☐ Salaried Non-Exempt	☐ Hourly Service
	(ship/rec, QA, maintenance)

YOUR OPINIONS (For each sentence give us your opinion—strongly agree, agree, disagree, or strongly disagree.)

SA   A   D   SD

☐   ☐   ☐   ☐   1. New people receive good orientation.

☐   ☐   ☐   ☐   2. When problems occur in my job, I have the freedom to solve them.

☐   ☐   ☐   ☐   3. Our company's future is very secure.

☐   ☐   ☐   ☐   4. My supervisor helps me solve problems that occur in my job.

☐   ☐   ☐   ☐   5. The equipment with which I work is usually in good condition.

≈

☐   ☐   ☐   ☐   59. I think my performance is judged fairly.

☐   ☐   ☐   ☐   60. Management cares about the well-being of employees.

What do you like best about the company?

_____

_____

_____

If you have any comments on any items, place the number of that item below, followed by your comments:

_____

_____

_____

_____

Table 9.5 Manager Follow-Up Survey

1. Have you noticed any positive improvements in performance among your direct reports who participated in the Sales Communication program?

   _____ Yes _____ No   Comment: _____

2. Do you think it was worth involving your salespeople in the Sales Communication program?

   _____ Yes _____ No   Comment: _____

3. Other Perceptions?

   Comment: _____

CONCLUSION

Perception results are an integral part of the Results Assessment System, along with performance and learning results. It is best to think of these three domains as independent and not to assume or speculate on any correlation among the three. There is enough research evidence to support the view that these three are largely independent.

If you are truly interested in performance results, do not use perception data. If you are truly interested in learning results, do not use perception data. If the questions you have relate to personal feelings, beliefs, impressions, or comprehension internal to participants or stakeholders, use perception data, and report the findings as such.

The bottom line is that perceptions can get in the way and can be easily manipulated, and yet they are very important. HRD professionals should be in the forefront of responsibly collecting and reporting perception results data.

KEY POINTS TO REMEMBER

▼

- A perception is a personal feeling, belief, impression, or comprehension (for example, of an object, event, or quality).
- Participant and stakeholder perceptions provide important alternative vantage points.
- Fundamental performance and learning results cannot be measured adequately through perceptions.
- Perception instruments require careful construction in terms of content validity, overall simplicity, and response format.
- Perceptions of processes can focus on affect or utility related to processes.
- Perceptions of outcomes need to focus on perceptions of actual outcomes.

CHAPTER 10

Reporting
Assessment Findings

Assessment Problem: How do you communicate results assessment findings clearly and succinctly to users? How do you make sound decisions with the assessment data?

▼

One output of the Results Assessment System should be better decisions about developing human resources. This chapter provides solutions to two key problems usually encountered when using results assessment data to make decisions for organizational improvement: communicating findings effectively and making accurate decisions from the data.

Effective communication of results assessment findings is essential if the findings are to be supported and used by decision makers outside the HRD function. Assessment reports, however, are often confusing and lengthy, and they often languish unread. The goal of the reporting step is to transform the data collected, which may be voluminous, into useful information. To accomplish this, a standard and compact Results Assessment Report is described in this chapter.

The second problem is more complex. If the results desired from the program do indeed occur, then all is well. A hidden problem emerges when the desired or expected results do not occur. The natural tendency is to conclude that the intervention was flawed—sometimes an incorrect conclusion. The HRD process is really a subsystem embedded in the larger organizational system. Thus, results that occur are the product of not only the intervention but of shifting or unaccounted-for performance variables in the organizational system. This chapter discusses key factors that should be considered to arrive at a sound interpretation of results assessment data.

RESULTS ASSESSMENT REPORTS

The Results Assessment Report is an executive summary of the effectiveness of a program (or set of identical interventions). The intention is that an HRD intervention be assessed in terms of its effectiveness and that the results be reported to the appropriate stakeholders in the organization.

Results Assessment Reports have a standard format, standard sections, and standard means of reporting data, and they are almost always short—generally two to four pages in length. The standard format offers several key advantages:

- Assessors are required to state their message concisely and clearly.
- Users become accustomed to seeing unfamiliar data presented in a consistent manner, which aids understanding.
- Decision makers can quickly grasp the essential facts about the effectiveness of interventions.

The Results Assessment Report is a summary report, intended to be very user friendly and useful to decision makers, managers, and participants. (Thus, there are available data exceeding those contained in the report. These additional data are retained and used for tracking and improving specific elements of the program and for responding to specific inquiries.)

The report has eight standard sections (Figure 10.1 contains a sample report):

1. Organization and program identification heading. This material provides the critical identification data of the program name, dates of the intervention, location, and number of participants. This intervention level identification information is how all data should be stored in the database. Repeated interventions can be combined into a cumulative report that should have an equally descriptive, yet unique, header.
2. Program purpose. This simple and direct statement, usually fifty words or fewer, describes the original state of results and the expected results. Reference is also made to the state of the five performance variables (mission/goal, systems design, capacity, motivation, and expertise) at the organizational, process, and/or individual and group levels.
3. Program description. A description of the program in fifty to seventy-five words contains the title, length, descriptive features in terms of content or method, and the immediate outcome.

Figure 10.1. Sample Results Assessment Report

(Company) Healthcare Sales Performance Consulting

Program:	"Communicating the (Company) Advantage"	Company Logo
Dates:	January–September, XXXX, 24 Groups	
Participants:	180 Healthcare Sales/Account managers	

Program Purpose

When a (Company) employee meets with a potential or existing customer, he or she creates a professional impression, builds a credible, trustworthy relationship, and communicates the value of (Company) with a direct emphasis on our medical management capabilities.

Program Description

"Communicating the (Company) Advantage" is an intensive two-day program that focuses on listening, questioning, and presentation skills. It is designed to improve sales associates' ability to communicate the "medical management capability" in a way that improves sales results. During the two-day program, sales managers co-facilitate by providing technical expertise and serving as communications coaches. Sales managers also are required to go through the program and to coach and evaluate sales associates back on the job.

Evaluation Summary

In summary, the "Communicating the (Company) Advantage" programs were very effective. The program exceeded its goals in all of the areas evaluated thus far, ten months following the first program. See page two for a further breakdown of these results and contact Sales Performance Consulting if you wish additional information.

Figure 10.1. Sample Results Assessment Report, Cont'd.

Performance	Goal Attainment
• Financial Results	409%

Learning
• Expertise	117%

Perception
• Participant Perception	149%
• Sponsor Perception	147%

Approval

VP of Performance Consulting   Date: M/D/YR

Distribution List

- President
- Senior VP of Sales and Marketing
- Senior VP of Human Resources
- VP of National Accounts
- VP of Human Resource Development
- Area Operating Officer

The evaluation of this program is reported according to the effectiveness domains of performance, learning, and perceptions.

Performance

The overarching goal of this program was to increase sales through communication and presentation skills. Listed below is a summary of sales attributed directly to this performance improvement program.

Business Results by Type of Sale		Financial Results in Terms of Total Premium Equivalent
2 Markets "Y" Business		$ 5,500,000
1 Dental		290,000
2 PPO Firms		2,000,000
18 Markets "X" Business		57,620,000
1 National Account		13,000,000
24 Sales	*Totals*	$78,410,000

DEVELOPING MEASURES OF RESULTS

Figure 10.1. Sample Results Assessment Report, Cont'd.

The business results reported at this point are taken from 48 responses as to sales attributed to the program. These responses come mostly from sales personnel who attended the program; however, some managers responded on behalf of their whole office. It is important to note that sales data have not been submitted by all offices.

The approximate profitability of the communication program is as follows: The average value of a single reported sale is $3,267,083; the average net profitability on a single sale is 3.0%, or $98,012/sale; the total profit for this group of sales is $2,352,300.

The direct program cost per group is approximately $12,000, or $288,000 for all twenty-four groups. The approximate return on investment (ROI) of this program is equal to the total profit divided by the total cost of the programs. The financial results goal is a 2:1 ROI within twelve months. The financial results obtained were 8.17:1 ROI, or 409% of goal, for this nine-month period. Exhibit A provides more detail on sales attributed thus far to this communication program.

If we assume the goal for the "business results" is to increase average sales by 5% per program participant per year, business results will be based on an increase in the number of target market firms sold per rep per year. The business results will not be available until twelve months following the program, when all sales have been accounted for.

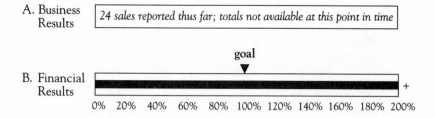

A. Business Results | 24 sales reported thus far; totals not available at this point in time

goal

B. Financial Results

0% 20% 40% 60% 80% 100% 120% 140% 160% 180% 200%

Figure 10.1. Sample Results Assessment Report, Cont'd.

While an approximation of ROI is a valuable measurement, the comments of participants add an additional dimension to the financial results. One sales manager's comments are listed below:

- "I am certain it [the program] has made a material difference in our results here in Boston. We have been awarded at least five substantial pieces of business since the initial training took place where the decision was made on the strength of our oral presentation. The five wins were as follows: Company A, $20 mil; Company B, $11 mil; Company C, $3 mil; Company D, $3 mil; Company E, existing client conversion to managed care.
- "In the case of Companies A, B, and E our competitor was Company X. In each case it came down to the oral presentation, as the metrics/financials for us and Company X were virtually the same. Preparation for the presentations was done using a lot of the principles and the process outlined in the communications training."
  —*(Name), Sales Manager, Boston*

Learning

Each participant was tested on "communication expertise." Managers used standardized rating forms to evaluate the expertise of participants on a multidimension, 3-point-per-dimension scale. The goal was a "meets clients' expectations" rating of 2 for each dimension. The average expertise for all groups immediately preceding training was 1.71, or 86% of goal. The average expertise for all groups at the end of the training was 2.12, or 106% of goal. The average expertise for all groups 60 days following training and coaching was 2.33, or 117% of goal. The overall improvement in communication expertise was 31% over the period. No paper-and-pencil "knowledge test" was used based on the assumption that the knowledge was required to succeed on the communication test of expertise.

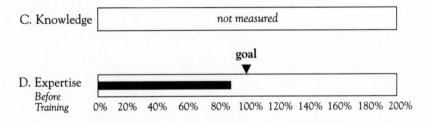

DEVELOPING MEASURES OF RESULTS

Figure 10.1. Sample Results Assessment Report, Cont'd.

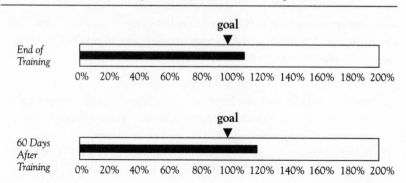

Perception

Participants and participant managers rated their perceptions of the communication program. The responses of 167 participants and their supervisors are reflected here. The goal for both measures was to have a positive average satisfaction rating of at least 2.5 on a 1–4 scale. The "participant satisfaction" results were 3.72, or 149% of goal. The "sponsor satisfaction" results were 3.68, or 147% of goal.

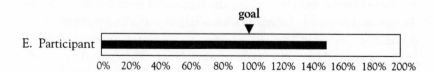

Figure 10.1. Sample Results Assessment Report, Cont'd.

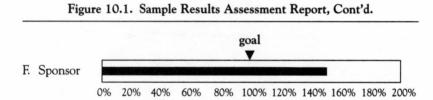

Participants in all areas expressed overwhelming enthusiasm and satisfaction with the program. Listed below are some of their comments:

- "Every (Company) employee should be subject to at least some aspects of this seminar."
  (Name), New York City Sales

- "As a Client Manager, I do not have the same opportunity to use my communication skills in selling 'new' cases. Instead, I use it in selling renewals, in selling additional 'Y' business, in solving customer issues, and working with my internal customers to resolve our clients' problems."
  (Name), Chicago Sales

- "I appreciate my company investing in *me* through this program."
  (Name), New York City Sales

- "This is a great program! There is nothing more important than communicating the vision!"
  (Name), Jacksonville Sales

- "It was definitely time well spent. I view it as an investment into our success."
  (Name), Chicago Sales

- "I am absolutely convinced that as a result of the CCA and follow-up training with Stump Speeches that my people are more impactful—that is, they can communicate our story more convincingly, more consistently than ever before. I have no doubt that those skills have impacted our ability to sell in the marketplace. On absolutely every case we sold, the skills training leveraged our ability to sell the case. Similarly, the training leveraged our ability to avoid losing our cases."
  (Name), Sales Manager, Florida

Suggestions for Improvement

The key suggestion for improvement is to follow up more vigorously on the utilization of the coaching form by the sales managers.

Figure 10.1. Sample Results Assessment Report, Cont'd.

Exhibit A

Sales Attributed to Communication Program

Number of Sales	Name of Sales Associate	Name of Account(s)	Premium Equivalent
2 PPO firms	Kathrine Parker, New York City	Account A Account B	$1,000,000 $1,000,000
4 target markets	William Maenner, Virginia	Account C Account D Account E Account F	$900,000 $400,000 $170,000 $400,000
4 target markets	James Thurston, Boston	Account G Account H Account I Account J	$3,000,000 $3,000,000 $20,000,000 $11,000,000
1 dental	Tom Salamone, Philadelphia	Account K	$290,000
2 target markets	Elizabeth Jensen, Carolina	Account L Account M	$3,500,000 $2,000,000

Reporting Assessment Findings

Figure 10.1. Sample Results Assessment Report, Cont'd.

Number of Sales	Name of Sales Associate	Name of Account(s)	Premium Equivalent
2 target markets	Greg Hill, Great Lakes	Account N Account O	$500,000 $350,000
1 target market	Gene Poor, Chicago	Account P	$2,500,000
4 target markets	Barbara Johnson, Miami	Account Q Account R Account S Account T	$8,400,000 (combined)
1 national account	George Strother, Carolina	Account U	$13,000,000
2 target markets	Christina Swanson, Tennessee	Account V Account W	$3,000,000 (combined)
1 target market	Finn Tavis, Birmingham	Account X	$4,000,000
		Total value	$78,410,000

Editor's note: The original report specifies the actual salesperson and account names.

4. Results summary. This is a simple presentation of each of the six assessment options selected and the percentage of attainment of the established goal within each (for example, financial results could be 200 percent of the goal, while expertise results could be 98 percent of goal).

5. Approval. Space is left for the signature of the appropriate person(s) ultimately responsible for the intervention.

6. Distribution list. This notes who should receive all reports related to this program. There is likely a short list of people who should receive assessment reports for all interventions and an additional list for each specific program. Together they make up the distribution list for a single report.

7. Assessment results. This is the largest single section of the report. The data are collected and reported in the effectiveness domains of performance (system and financial results), learning (knowledge and expertise results), and perception (participant and stakeholder results). We recommend that all data be converted into a standard "percentage of goal" scale to reduce the data interpretation to the simplest level. For example, if the participant perception goal is to achieve an average participant perception rating of acceptable or higher, the goal is 2.5 on a 1–4 scale, with 2.5 representing 100 percent of the goal. If the average was 2.0 (below the goal), the percentage of goal attained would be reported as 75 percent. A reaction perception average of 3.0 would be 125 percent of the goal. The purpose of this simplified percentage of goal reporting method is to ensure the accurate interpretation of the evaluation data by the largest number of people as they view this report and all subsequent reports.

8. Improvement proposal. The last section of the Results Assessment Report is a statement of twenty-five to one hundred words that focuses on the assessment results in the context of the purpose and the description of the program and what needs to be done to improve performance.

BARRIERS TO MAKING SOUND
DECISIONS FROM RESULTS DATA

Experienced professionals know that making sound decisions requires more than simply looking at results data. Let us say that you have measured the results of a new HRD intervention. The data indicate that learning did occur, but performance results at the individual and process level did not. What decision do you make about the program? Using only the data you have collected, the only decision possible is that the HRD intervention was flawed. Is that decision correct?

The answer is maybe. Advanced models of performance analysis (Swanson, 1996) and HRD effectiveness (Holton, 1996) clearly indicate that a multiple of variables drive and affect results. For example, suppose that an employee returns to the job and tries to use new techniques learned in training, only to have the supervisor require that old methods be used instead? In that case, results measurement would show positive learning results but poor performance results, even though the training program was excellent.

In this section, we present a framework for analyzing barriers to results that lie outside the intervention itself. Failure to account for the performance variables in the up-front analysis as well as in the follow-up assessment can lead to incorrect decisions about interventions. When combined with results data, this reflective information helps in making sound decisions.

Barriers to Results

The performance diagnosis process (Figure 10.2; see Swanson, 1996) and the supporting performance diagnosis matrix of enabling questions (see Figure 6.1) are the best means of understanding the avenue to results and in revealing barriers that arise along the way.

We have defined HRD as a process of developing or unleashing human expertise for the purpose of improving performance. It is our

DEVELOPING MEASURES OF RESULTS

Figure 10.2. The Performance Diagnosis Process

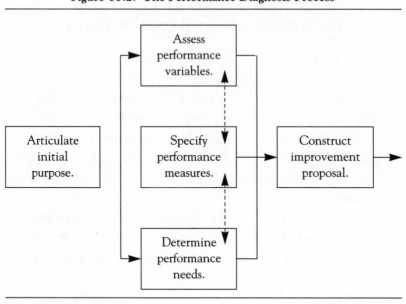

Source: Swanson, 1996.

contention that achieving this goal requires HRD professionals at the front-end analysis phase to disconnect temporarily from its two primary tools: organization development (unleashing expertise) and personnel training and development (developing expertise). This is done to allow the HRD professional to gain a broad view and analysis of the organization (a human system), the larger context in which it functions, and all of the organizational processes working to achieve core organizational goals. In addition, HRD professionals should be proposing partnership interventions that go beyond HRD. And they should be perfectly willing to say they cannot contribute significantly to the desired results when they cannot reasonably do so.

Once HRD does get involved in developing or unleashing human expertise, HRD professionals have a unique role related to their understanding of learning—attaining knowledge and expertise.

Following is a brief description of each group of barriers related to learning that is turned into performance and to learning itself. Each is illustrated with a figure that includes a checklist of audit questions you can use to decide if the barrier might exist in your situation

The first step in converting learning into performance is for a worker's knowledge and expertise to have an impact on his or her individual performance on the job. In the literature this is often referred to as *transfer of learning* or *transfer of training*. Transfer research (Bates, Holton, and Seyler, 1997) has clearly shown that for knowledge and expertise (wherever and however it is developed) to lead to performance, the environment in which it is used must be receptive to it. In fact, the environment to which a worker enters typically is a more powerful influence than the learning itself when it comes to performance.

We can look at the barriers to using knowledge and expertise in the workplace divided into the three topics (Holton, Bates, Ruona, and Leimbach, 1998; Holton, Bates, and Seyler, 1997):

• Ability to use knowledge and expertise. The first group of factors deals with the worker's ability to use his or her learning on the job (Figure 10.3). Ability can be a barrier in two arenas: on the job and in the learning event (discussed in the next section). On the job, the lack of opportunity to use one's learning may exist, or a lack of personal capacity to try out the learning may inhibit its use.

• Motivation to use learning. Motivational factors comprise the second group (Figure 10.4). Workers, in viewing their own learning, need to have both the ability to apply knowledge and the motivation to do so. Motivation has two components: the beliefs that expended effort will change performance and that changed performance leads to outcomes they value. Workers also need to have high performance self-efficacy, that is, the general belief that they can use learning to change their performance.

**Figure 10.3. Example for Identifying Potential Barriers
in the Ability to Use Knowledge and Expertise**

Potential Barrier	Definition	Audit Questions
Opportunity to use learning	The extent to which workers are provided with or obtain resources and tasks on the job enabling them to use their knowledge and expertise	❏ Do workers have opportunities on the job to apply their knowledge and expertise? ❏ Do they have the resources needed to use their learning (equipment, information, materials and supplies)? ❏ Are there enough funds to use learning? ❏ Are there enough supporting people to allow workers to implement their learning?
Personal capacity for transfer	The extent to which individuals have the time, energy, and mental space in their work lives to make changes required to use learning on the job	❏ Are workers' workloads adjusted to practice their expertise? ❏ Do workers have the personal energy to devote to new methods? ❏ Are workers' stress levels already so high they cannot cope with more change?

**Figure 10.4. Example for Identifying Potential Barriers
in the Motivation to Use Knowledge and Expertise**

Potential Barrier	*Definition*	*Audit Questions*
Motivation to transfer learning	Are workers motivated to utilize their knowledge and expertise in their work?	❏ Do learners feel better able to perform? ❏ Do they plan to use their knowledge and expertise? ❏ Do workers believe their learning will help them to perform on the job more effectively?
Performance self-efficacy	Workers' general belief that they are able to change their performance when they want to	❏ Do workers feel confident and self-assured about applying their abilities in their jobs? ❏ Can they overcome obstacles that hinder the use of their knowledge and skills?
Transfer effort— performance expectations	The expectation that effort devoted to use learning will lead to changes in	❏ Do workers believe that applying their knowledge and expertise will improve their performance? ❏ Do workers believe that investing effort to use new learning has made a difference in the past? ❏ Do workers believe that doing so will affect future productivity and effectiveness?

Figure 10.4. Example for Identifying Potential Barriers in the Motivation to Use Knowledge and Expertise, Cont'd.

Potential Barrier	Definition	Audit Questions
Performance—outcomes expectations	The expectation that changes in job performance will lead to outcomes valued by the individual	❑ Do workers believe the application of knowledge and expertise learned will lead to personal recognition that they value?
		❑ Does the organization demonstrate the link between development, performance, and recognition?
		❑ Does the organization clearly articulate performance expectations and recognize individuals when they do well?
		❑ Are individuals rewarded for effective and improved performance?
		❑ Does the organization create an environment in which individuals feel positive about performing well?

• Work environments designed to use knowledge and expertise. The third area consists of work environment factors—system designs and rewards. Research consistently shows that the work environment can be a tremendous barrier to workers' using their knowledge and expertise (Figure 10.5). Three factors deal with the worker's relationship with his or her supervisor: feedback or performance coaching about the use of the learning, the amount of support the worker gets for using the learning, and the extent to which the supervisor actively opposes the use of new knowledge and expertise. Two factors deal with the work group: the support that peers provide for using new approaches and the extent to which the group norm is open to change. And two factors deal with the reward systems: the extent to which the outcomes for the person are positive or negative.

Barriers to Learning

Suppose that results data show that learning was not acceptable, either because it was too low or because no learning took place. One reason might be that the learning event itself was flawed. It is beyond the scope of this book to analyze all the possible influences within the learning event that can affect learning outcomes. Other books offer excellent discussions about effective learning strategies (see, for example, Davis and Davis, 1998; Gagne and Medsker, 1996; Knowles, Holton, and Swanson, 1998).

Our concern here is with factors that may lead one to conclude wrongly that the reason for poor learning results is that the learning experience itself was flawed. Following are the key factors that can influence learning outcomes but are not actually part of the learning experience itself:

Motivation to learn. Learners who lack the motivation to learn, even when the content is good, are a key barrier to learning (Figure 10.6). Some people have low levels of motivation

DEVELOPING MEASURES OF RESULTS

**Figure 10.5. Example for Identifying Potential Barriers in
the Work Environment to Use Knowledge and Expertise**

Potential Barrier	Definition	Audit Questions
Supervisor feedback/ performance coaching	Formal and informal indicators from an organization about an individual's job performance	❑ Do individuals receive constructive input and assistance when applying new abilities or attempting to improve work performance? ❑ Do they receive informal and formal feedback from people in their work environment (peers, employees, colleagues)?
Supervisor/ manager support	The extent to which managers support and reinforce learning on the job	❑ Do managers clarify performance expectations after HRD experiences? ❑ Do they identify opportunities to apply knowledge and expertise? ❑ Do they set realistic goals based on new learning? ❑ Do they work with individuals on problems encountered while applying new learning? ❑ Do they provide recognition when individuals successfully apply new learning?

**Figure 10.5. Example for Identifying Potential Barriers in
the Work Environment to Use Knowledge and Expertise, Cont'd.**

Potential Barrier	Definition	Audit Questions
Supervisor/ manager opposition	The extent to which individuals perceive negative responses from managers when applying new learning	❏ Do managers oppose the use of new knowledge and expertise? ❏ Do managers use techniques different from those learned by workers? ❏ Do they provide negative feedback when individuals successfully apply new learning on the job?
Work group support	The extent to which peers reinforce and support use of learning on the job	❏ Do peers mutually identify and implement opportunities to apply new knowledge and expertise? ❏ Do peers encourage the use of or expect the application of new learning? ❏ Do peers display patience with difficulties associated with applying new learning? ❏ Do peers demonstrate appreciation for the use of new expertise?

Figure 10.5. Example for Identifying Potential Barriers in
the Work Environment to Use Knowledge and Expertise, Cont'd.

Potential Barrier	Definition	Audit Questions
Openness to change	Are work groups perceived by individuals to resist or discourage the use of new knowledge and expertise?	❏ Do work groups actively resist change? ❏ Are they willing to invest energy to change? ❏ Do they support individuals who use new techniques?
Positive personal rewards	The degree to which applying learning on the job leads to outcomes that are positive for the individual	❏ Does the use of new learning lead to rewards such as increased productivity and work effectiveness, increased personal satisfaction, additional respect, a salary increase or reward, the opportunity to further career development plans, or the opportunity to advance in the organization?
Personal outcomes—negative	The extent to which individuals believe that applying their knowledge and expertise will lead to negative outcomes	❏ Does the use of new learning lead to negative outcomes such as reprimands, penalties, peer resentment, too much new work, or the likelihood of not getting a raise if newly acquired expertise is used?

**Figure 10.6. Examples for Identifying
Potential Barriers in Motivation to Learn**

Potential Barrier	Definition	Audit Questions
Previous experiences using learning on the job	The extent to which previous experiences in attempting to use learning to change performance have been successful	❑ Have learners been discouraged by previous failed attempts to use learning? ❑ Are the transfer factors listed above sufficient to support learning?
Learner readiness	The extent to which individuals are prepared to enter and participate in learning	❑ Did individuals have the opportunity to provide input prior to the learning intervention? ❑ Did they know what to expect? ❑ Did they understand how training was related to job-related development and work performance?
General motivation to learn	The extent to which learners are motivated to learn and grow	❑ Does the organization encourage and support continual learning and growth? ❑ Have learners been successful learning this type of material previously?
Confidence	The extent to which learners have the confidence and self-esteem about learning	❑ Are learners confident of their ability to master new material? ❑ Do the learners have the support they need from the organization?

because of negative previous experiences using learning on the job. In other cases, basic principles that improve learner readiness for learning are not used, leaving the learner confused or resentful. Learners also vary widely in their general motivation to learn, with some having a strong learning drive and others who do not like to learn. (Often this is a function of their lack of confidence in being effective learners.)

Ability to learn. The general presumption is that every learner has the ability to perform the learning tasks required. Increasingly, however, organizations are finding this is not the case. Employees may not have the general ability to learn, or they may lack the skills necessary to learn new types of material. The learning content itself may have little perceived content validity, making it difficult for learners to understand how it relates to their jobs. Or it may be taught with low transfer design so that learners have little chance of turning knowledge into workplace expertise. Finally, some workers simply lack the basic workplace skills such as reading, writing, or listening skills to be effective learners. (See Figure 10.7.)

CONCLUSION

Reporting results is the critical last step in the Results Assessment System. Those processes in organizations that regularly submit reports of effort and results gain attention, support, and respect. We regularly hear the logistical and administrative excuses for not reporting results. We find this talk indefensible. The Results Assessment System is neatly defined and framed, and it culminates with concise and consistently formatted reports. No reports mean no results in the minds of many organizational decision makers. Do not ignore this last step.

**Figure 10.7. Examples for Identifying
Potential Barriers in Learning Ability**

Potential Barrier	Definition	Audit Questions
General ability to learn	The extent to which learners have basic learning ability	❏ Does the learner have the general aptitude to learn the material?
		❏ Does the learner need refresher training on prerequisite material?
Learning skills	The extent to which an individual's learning skills are congruent with the learning tasks	❏ Is the learning task considerably different from that previously encountered (e.g., computer-based learning versus instructor led?)
		❏ Does the learning require a higher level of learning skill than the individual possesses or has used previously?
Perceived content validity	The extent to which the participants judge the learning content to reflect job requirements accurately	❏ Are the skills and knowledge taught similar enough to performance expectations to be viewed as credible?
		❏ Are they what the individual needs in order to perform more effectively?
		❏ Are the instructional methods, aids, and equipment used similar to those used in the work environment?

Figure 10.7. Examples for Identifying Potential Barriers in Learning Ability, Cont'd.

Potential Barrier	Definition	Audit Questions
Transfer design	The extent to which learning has been designed to match job requirements and give participants the ability to transfer learning to job application	❏ Is the learning designed to link it clearly to on-the-job performance? ❏ Do examples, activities, and exercises clearly demonstrate how to apply new knowledge and skills? ❏ Are the teaching methods used similar to the work environment?
Basic workplace skills (reading, writing, etc.)	The extent to which learners have the basic skills necessary to perform learning tasks	❏ Does the learner have the basic workplace skills needed to learn work-related material? ❏ Does the learner need remedial education?

KEY POINTS TO REMEMBER

▼

- Results assessment findings must be carefully communicated if they are to be supported and used by stakeholders. A structured report format helps ensure consistency, conciseness, and clarity.
- Results reports contain standard sections: organization and program identification heading, program purpose, program description, results summary, approval, distribution list, assessment results, and improvement proposal.
- Reports contain data within each of the selected six options of the performance, learning, and perception domains. The data are summarized for each option in terms of percentage of the goal attainment.
- Data alone can lead to incorrect decisions about interventions when results do not occur. In order to make valid decisions when desired results do not occur, a variety of system factors that can be barriers to results must be examined.

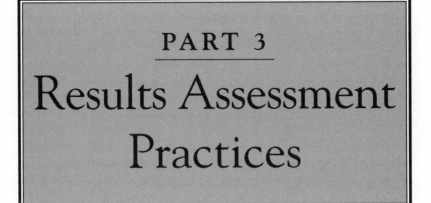

PART 3

Results Assessment Practices

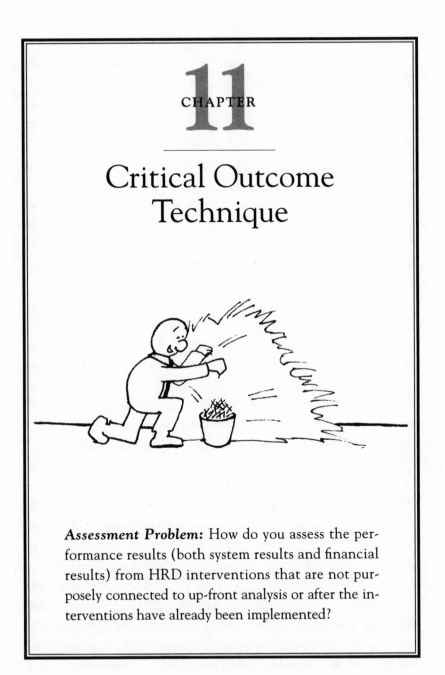

CHAPTER

11

Critical Outcome Technique

Assessment Problem: How do you assess the performance results (both system results and financial results) from HRD interventions that are not purposely connected to up-front analysis or after the interventions have already been implemented?

189

▼

The Critical Outcome Technique (COT) represents an important development in follow-up assessment of performance results to interventions not having direct and planned connections to performance improvement (Mattson, 1999; Swanson and Mattson, 1997). Other than the COT, the primary avenue for demonstrating performance results is through a systematic improvement process (including up-front performance analysis and follow-up systematic evaluation). In contrast, the COT begins after the intervention has been implemented. (The COT is similar to the Critical Incident Technique in that both function within the milieu of an ongoing organization. The COT yields critical outcome performance data that are verifiable and quantifiable.)

Demonstrating performance results is considered difficult because of problems associated with establishing causality. Accordingly, results assessment techniques that are rooted in "before versus after" experimental research methodologies are often proposed (Grove and Ostroff, 1990; Arvey and Cole, 1989; Goldstein, 1986). However, the practical utility of these methods is questionable. In the end, every assessment should represent a situation-specific effort that meets the needs of program stakeholders (Cronbach, 1982).

Most professionals would agree that performance results both influence and are influenced by the sponsoring organization. For this reason, many professionals advocate that interventions be analyzed in terms of improving the performance of the broader system (Rummler and Brache, 1995). To do this, they advocate up-front analysis to understand and identify performance improvement requirements and cite it as the most crucial part of the performance improvement process (Sleezer, 1989). In these instances, results assessment is based directly on performance objectives determined in the up-front analysis. The performance requirements are the basis for both performance objectives of the intervention and the follow-up assessment of their attainment.

In contrast to this rigorous approach, many programs and assessments are often based on general assumptions about perceived needs, not rigorous analysis. In other instances, needs are determined on a case-by-case basis. For example, many companies offer regularly scheduled development programs—such as general computer training programs—that employees can sign up for on an individual basis.

These programs are not linked to predetermined performance outcomes for specific groups or individuals, and usually do not have performance assessments of the organizational usefulness of the program. If they are evaluated at all, it is typically at the level of participant reactions. Thus, in spite of all the discussion about performance results, very little assessment of performance outcomes actually takes place.

THE CRITICAL OUTCOME TECHNIQUE MODEL

A review of the literature used as the basis of developing the COT illustrates the following problems in the area of performance assessment:

- Assessment of the results often requires complex designs, which are very difficult to implement in practice.
- The optimal techniques for assessing programs in the context of the larger system in which they are designed to operate rely on rigorous front-end analyses. Most organizations, however, are not able to allocate the large investments of resources required for such analyses.
- The theoretical models the profession currently uses to guide assessment lack the technique necessary to evaluate outcomes in an efficient fashion.
- The underlying assumption of such models is that the program was instrumental in achieving a given objective or set of

objectives. In the absence of an analysis of performance requirements, this assumption is tenuous at best.

These themes point to the desirability of having a procedure for
demonstrating value-added outcomes of HRD programs that does
not require front-end analysis. Such a technique should be relatively
easy to use yet generate valid and reliable data about the actual outcomes of a program. Additionally, the procedure should be flexible
enough to be used after a program has been completed in the
absence of front-end analysis data regarding program objectives.

The model of the COT in Figure 11.1 shows five components.

Outcome Definition

The primary question of concern in this phase is, "What were the
intended critical outcomes of this program?" Individuals associated
with the approval and development of the program are used as the
data source because they are most likely to be aware of the intended
objectives of the program.

Follow-up questions are used to operationalize the definitions of
outcomes. It is important to distinguish between outcome statements
and activity statements in the evaluation of programs. Activity statements contain nonspecific language—for example, "The objective
of this program was to build partnerships between departments." In
contrast, when outcome statements are operationalized, such statements can answer the question, "How will you know when the out-

Figure 11.1. Model of the Critical Outcome Technique

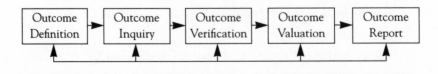

come has been achieved?" In the previous example, an operationalized outcome statement would be something like this: "The intended
outcome of this program was an increase in sales through improved
communication." *Metrics* (ways of assessing if the outcome has
occurred) must also be defined in this phase because they will be
needed to assess the program's success.

Outcome Inquiry

The main question in this phase is, "What were the actual outcomes
of the program?" Actual outcomes of the program may be intended
(as defined by program sponsors) or unintended. Program participants are the data collection source in this phase because they have
the most knowledge about how their behavior, and hence outcomes,
was affected by a program. The preferred data collection technique
in this instance is an interview or focus group. However, if the outcome metric is clearly defined, it may be adequate simply to send out
a questionnaire to gather data.

Outcome Verification

This phase addresses the questions, "Did the outcome(s) really occur
as reported by the participants?" and "To what degree would the out-
come(s) have occurred in the absence of the program?" Program
stakeholders best answer the first question. For instance, in the case
of a sales communication improvement program, a sales manager
might be asked to verify that a sale actually occurred as reported by
a program participant.

Regarding the attributability of the outcome to the program, we
encounter all kinds of methodological difficulties that are best addressed by rigorous basic research methodologies. In response to such
concerns, we must remember the arguments put forth by Cronbach
(1982) and Patton (1990) that program evaluation does not represent

a rigid representation of the "truth." More appropriately, program assessment represents an artful effort to produce information on which decisions can be made. In this sense, estimates of the attributability of an outcome of a program should be reasonably accurate rather than exactly on the money. Consulting more than one data source is recommended to ensure that estimates are closer to being accurate representations. It is also recommended that such sources be investigated independently, to avoid any biased estimates due to social desirability or groupthink.

Outcome Valuation

In this phase, the primary question of interest is, "How much is this outcome worth?" admittedly, a difficult judgment to make. However, as in the case of attributability, more estimates of the value of an outcome are better because they provide the basis for reflection and judgment. For example, multiple estimates of costs avoided by retaining rather than replacing an employee will likely lead to a more accurate number. If the outcome does not have an assignable financial value, it must be valued in some other way. For instance, if the outcome of a program was a reduction in the number of customer complaints about a product, then the approximate number of complaints reduced should be noted. Top management might be willing to assign a dollar value as to what this is worth.

Outcome Report

The final phase of the COT is the production of an outcome report, which in the spirit of Cronbach (1982), Patton (1990), and Brinkerhoff (1995), represents an attempt to satisfy the needs of the customer of the report. For instance, if the report is intended for a general audience, it is probably best not to include elaborate descriptions of reported outcomes. With every outcome report, data to back up the report, if necessary, should be accessible.

USING THE COT IN THE SALES COMMUNICATION CASE

Critical outcomes can be thought of as performance outcomes in the forms of system results, which are then turned into financial results. For example, the business result of increasing market share by 5 percent could be converted into number of sales times the financial value of each sale. In this example, the system results can be converted into money equivalents and then expressed in terms of financial results.

In the sales communication improvement case, the critical outcome was increased sales. The company had actual sales. The purpose of this variation on the sales communication improvement case study is to illustrate the application of the COT. This involves the assessment of critical outcomes from a communication improvement program for sales personnel in a major insurance company. The sales force sells insurance plans to employers and for this illustration the numbers of sales per year are small (10–20 per year) and each sale is large ($380,000 average). The performance improvement intervention in this case included training, changes in the work process, and a revised performance appraisal system. This was provided to over a hundred sales personnel at various sites throughout the nation over six-month period.

Utilizing the COT, it was determined that the critical outcome was increased sales. The company has a system for tracking sales by salesperson, office, region, and product, plus standard gross and net financial measures per sale. The connection between available financial measures and the interventions of this case was not known at the onset and became clear through the application of the COT.

The decision was to have participants identify sales they attributed to the program and to do this sixty days following the effort. Salespeople and their supervisors were asked to report on any sales or portion of sales they attributed to the communication program. The vice president of sales assumed the position that these estimates would be underestimates, and the specific sale had to be recorded if there were any questions about the backup data. Thus, these were not perceptions of performance. Rather, they were verifiable sales cautiously attributed to the intervention. The total number of attributed sales was multiplied by the net worth of an average sale. A meeting with the comptroller yielded this figure following an exploratory conversation about available financial data. The direct cost of the intervention was compared to the net profit from the reported sales attributable to the sales communication improvement program to determine the ROI. In this case the increased value of the sales for the first six months was $4,590,000, and the cost of the intervention was $610,000. This exceeds a seven-to-one ROI in six months $(4,590,000/610,000 = 7.52)$.

The COT functioned effectively and efficiently in this case. The internal challenges from corporate decision makers came in two areas: (1) the questioning of financial worth of the selected critical outcome and (2) the questioning of the validity of the core critical outcome data. Both were sustained. The comptroller established the financial worth of each sale—the critical outcome. Her credibility and lack of bias around the intervention validated the COT effort. In terms of the validity of the sales data, each sale was clearly detailed in the results report (verifiable) and judged by both the participant and participant's manager to be a result of the intervention (attributable).

APPLYING THE COT TO GENERAL-CONTENT TRAINING PROGRAMS

Will general training programs produce critical outcomes, and will the COT be able to locate them?

This section illustrates the application of the critical outcome definition (first phase) of the COT to six general-content corporate training programs (Mattson, Quartana, and Swanson, 1998).

The description of HRD programs and the stated or implied objectives of each are fundamental to deriving the outcome definition—the first phase of the COT. The outcome definition is the basis for the execution of the COT. Following are the program description, objectives, and outcome definition for six training programs, derived from program documents after the programs were already implemented. They serve to illustrate the starting point for implementing step 1 of the COT model.

Overview of Insurance Business: A three-phase program offered once a year consisting of a one-day kickoff session, two months of advance assignments carried out as a team, and a final three-day seminar of team report-outs, lectures by senior manager subject matter experts on eight topics, and discussions.

- Stated Purpose: To provide a forum for high-potential people to learn from senior management and from one another about the principal external and internal drivers that affect the business of a shareholder-owned, multiple-line insurance company. To explore how the corporation competes for both customers and capital to create long-term shareholder value.
- Outcome Definition: Has a critical outcome (good or bad), such as new strategic initiatives, occurred in your work setting as a result of your participation in the Overview of Insurance Business program?

Essentials of Leadership: A three-day program consolidating three former Essentials of Leadership programs into one. The program is an extension of the Basics of Leadership Development (BOLD) initiative and is geared to experienced managers.

- Implied Purpose: To provide knowledge and skills training for experienced managers in the areas of performance management, communication, and coaching.

- Outcome Definition: Has a critical outcome (good or bad), such as department effectiveness measures, occurred in your work setting as a result of your participation in the Essentials of Leadership program?

The Dale Carnegie Course: An off-the-shelf motivational course on personal development through assigned readings, class exercises, and speaking assignments.

- Implied Purpose: To develop or improve personal traits and skills, including performance and effectiveness, leadership, memory and powers of concentration, courage and confidence, and effective communication, in addition to learning how to control stress and excessive worry.
- Outcome Definition: Has a critical outcome (good or bad), such as personal performance ratings, occurred in your work setting as a result of your participation in the Dale Carnegie Course?

Diversity Awareness: An interactive one and one-half-day non-confrontational and inclusive workshop consisting of prereading assignments, small group work, videos, and large group discussions, activities, and interactions.

- Stated Purpose: To heighten selected investment management and investment law employees' awareness of diversity and diversity issues.
- Outcome Definition: Has a critical outcome (good or bad), such as improved work group effectiveness or a reduction of complaints and/or filed grievances, occurred in your work setting as a result of your participation in the Diversity Awareness program?

Finance for Non-Financial Professionals: "Enjoyable" approach to learning about finance using a manual having cartoon figures and clear, easy-to-understand examples, lectures, and activities to practice and test what has been learned throughout the course.

- Stated Purpose: To educate attorneys and paralegals on how the corporation makes money: the fundamentals of finance, accounting principles, and business units as capital.
- Outcome Definition: Has a critical outcome (good or bad), such as legal decisions that affect financial outcomes, occurred in your work setting as a result of your participation in the Finance for Non-Financial Professionals program?

Project Management Certificate Program: The program is composed of four individual curriculums that support the overall objective of professionalizing the role of project managers in the corporation. Curricula include a Project Management Certificate Program, a Coaching Certificate Program, a Management/Customer Workshop, and Project: Quickstarts.

- Stated Purpose: To improve corporate staff project management capabilities through training, on-the-job coaching, and exposure to (external) project management experts and ideas. Specifically, it provides specific training in the nine major areas of project management (as identified in Project Management Body of Knowledge). The training focuses on the "what" (process, etc.).
- Outcome Definition: Has a critical outcome (good or bad), such as project cost overruns and meeting project deadlines, occurred in your work setting as a result of your participation in the Project Management Certificate?

These examples further illustrate the results assessment through the COT. Producing an outcome definition for an HRD intervention, the critical first phase of the COT, answers the basic question, "What were the intended critical outcomes of this program?"

CONCLUSION

The Critical Outcome Technique (COT) has been proved to be a workable alternative to traditional assessment. With little or no up-front analysis guiding an intervention, the COT can produce reliable and valid performance data after the fact. These performance outcome data are almost always underestimates of the true results of interventions. Even with partial performance outcome data, the cost of most interventions is quite modest, and the financial worth of performance results will end up more than justifying the investment.

KEY POINTS TO REMEMBER

▼

- The COT demonstrates value-added outcomes of development programs without requiring front-end analysis.
- The COT is flexible enough to be used after a program has been completed in the absence of front-end analysis data and program objectives.
- The primary question of the first COT phase is, "What were the intended critical outcomes of this program?"
- Outcomes attributed to a development program must be verified.
- The COT culminates in a financial ROI for the program being assessed.

CHAPTER

12

Auditing Program Practices
and Effectiveness

Assessment Problem: How do I get an overall assessment of the effectiveness of an HRD function or department in terms of its work process and program outcomes?

▼

Auditing is a familiar process to businesspeople, particularly those in the accounting and financial world, but it is relatively unfamiliar to HRD professionals. The basic question underlying an audit is whether what was actually done matched the intentions. An audit is essentially a review by an expert. The audit process has these core components:

- A subject matter expert, usually from outside the organization.
- A set of materials, documentation, or practices that are made available for review (generally a sample of the work being done rather than everything).
- Standards against which practices are audited. These may be generally accepted practices or carefully defined and documented ones. They may also be expert opinion.
- A process for incorporating findings into organizational practices.

The issue of standards deserves additional discussion because there are many different approaches that can work. Table 12.1 summarizes several strategies, all of which have their advantages.

Table 12.1. Sources of Standards for Audits

Standard Type	Examples	Advantages
• Broad flexible standards	ISO 9001 Baldrige quality criteria	Allow flexibility of intepretation by individual organizations
• Detailed generic standards	Instructional design Professional competencies	Provide standards of best practice across industries
• Detailed, industry-specific standards	Nuclear industry standards Organization's own standards	Provide standards of best practice within industries
• Expert opinion	Industry experts University professors Consultants	Often provides more depth of experience and expertise

An audit is an assessment against some standard. It can be used in the following ways:

- An easy way to get started with results assessment if resources are not available for ongoing assessment
- A low-threat way to introduce results assessment into an organization
- A quick way to examine a lot of interventions to see which ones warrant further assessment
- A way to get an outside expert's perspective on the organization's practices

Obviously the success of an audit depends on the process that is followed and the expertise that the subject matter expert possesses.

THE AUDITING PROCESS

Although the specific steps can vary, an audit usually encompasses the following process elements:

1. Establish the specific purpose and process of the audit with stakeholders. It is important to come to agreement with stakeholders early in the process about components of the audit. These should include the following:
   - Understanding organizational mission and goals
   - Organizational units to be audited and key personnel
   - Purpose and process of the audit
2. Plan the audit. It is important to have a thorough written plan for the audit and that it be shared with all those involved.
   - Determine the standards against which practices will be compared.
   - Determine the method of data collection.
   - Schedule the audit time line (including dates, personnel and data requirements).

3. Conduct the audit. It is important that the audit be conducted professionally.
   • Communicate with all those involved in the audit process.
   • Adhere to the audit schedule and time line.
4. Draft the audit report. It is important to consider carefully and integrate all relevant findings in the report.
   • Structure the report in the same way as the audit process and the audit standards used.
   • Review the audit report with the primary client or other stakeholder and revise as appropriate.
5. Finalize the audit report. It is important that the final report be able to stand alone.
   • Incorporate appropriate stakeholder comments into the report.
   • Provide a one-page summary at the front of the report along with a transmittal letter.
6. Auditors present the report to appropriate stakeholders. It is best to present the findings so questions can be answered and the results used to begin a collaborative conversation about how to apply the findings.
   • Submit reports to key personnel prior to the meeting.
   • Have a short formal presentation and an open discussion.
7. Integrate the audit report into strategic plans and actions. Audits are not worth much unless they are incorporated into organizational planning.
   • Make suggestions as to how the audit information can be used.
   • Follow up with key personnel as to the actions they have taken as a result of the audit.

HRD AUDITING STRATEGY

One approach that we have used successfully is to structure the audit using the five-phase general HRD process model described in Chapter Two. The purpose of this approach is to create an audit strategy that is simple enough to be easily implemented but still be theoretically sound. This strategy is a high-level audit of interventions to spot systemic problems and trouble points deserving further assessment. It can be applied to any HRD department, function, or set of interventions.

HRD Audit Framework

Each of the five phases of the HRD process model (analyze, propose, create, implement, and assess) was further divided into two subphases, for a total of ten foci for the audit. In addition, the question of HRD leadership is also raised and serves as the sixth major auditing category. The components of this framework are as follows:

1. *Analyze*—A process used for determining performance requirements that call for interventions, as well as how learning requirements were identified.
   1.1. Diagnosis of performance requirements (system goals and financial)
   1.2. Documentation of learning requirements (knowledge and expertise)

2. *Propose*—An examination of the analysis data in selecting and designing the proposed intervention.
   2.1. Intervention design (overall design and rationale)
   2.2. Detailed design (specific details of design)

3. *Create*—Development or procurement of the program materials created to support the intervention.
   3.1. Leader materials
   3.2. Participant materials

4. *Implement*—The management and logistics of implementing the program or intervention in the organization as well as the delivery of the program itself and the conduct within it.
   4.1. Program management
   4.2. Program delivery

5. *Assess*—The process used to assess intervention results, including performance, learning, and perceptions, and the reporting of those results.
   5.1. Performance, learning, and perception outcomes
   5.2. Reporting results

In addition to auditing the five phases for individual programs or a group of programs, it is critical that the leaders of the HRD function be audited in terms of the key questions related to their role:

6. *Leadership*—An examination of the extent to which leadership of the HRD function is effective in terms of evidence of policies, systems, and management.
   6.1. Policy
   6.2. Systems
   6.3. Management

Applying the Framework

The HRD audit framework focuses on the substance of the audit, while the seven-step audit process conceptually guides the sequence of the audit activity. Following are recommended steps for applying the audit process and the HRD audit framework:

1. Select the department, function, or intervention for auditing.
2. Select a recognized HRD expert as the auditor. The expert must know what best practices in the field are
3. Decide if the audit will be based on an on-site visit plus documentation or documentation only.

4. Have the expert auditor rate each intervention as "high," "medium," or "low" on each HRD framework dimension using the following definitional levels:
   - High = consistent evidence/good practice
   - Medium = some evidence/marginal practice
   - Low = no evidence/poor practice
5. Document specific reasons for each rating, for all ratings, and particularly for low ratings. These observations will become part of the narrative report.
6. Summarize the ratings for each program and each dimension into a table, as shown in Figure 12.1.
7. Based on the ratings, determine the overall ratings for the following categories:
   - Each intervention or program (horizontally in the table)
   - Each dimension (vertically in the table)
   - The overall set of interventions or programs being audited

REPORTING AUDIT RESULTS

The report to management and stakeholders should minimally include the following components:

1. A description of the program or interventions
2. For each audit dimension, the key findings from the audit that support the rating
3. A summary of the report:
   - The summary rating table (see Figure 12.1)
   - Overall strengths and areas for improvement based on the interventions or programs audited
4. An appendix that describes the audit process and the audit standards used

Figure 12.1. Sample Audit Rating Summary Form

HRD Process → / HRD Program ↓	1. Analyze		2. Propose		3. Create		4. Implement		5. Assess		Summary Rating
	Performance 1.1	Learning 1.2	Overall 2.1	Detail 2.2	Leader 3.1	Participant 3.2	Manage 4.1	Deliver 4.2	Outcomes 5.1	Reporting 5.2	
Essentials of Management	L	M	H	H	H	H	H	H	M	H	H
Financial, Marketing and Strategy: Overview	L	L	M	L	M	L	L	M	L	L	L
Systems Management Certificate Program	L	H	H	M	L	M	H	H	M	L	M
Summary Rating	L	M	H	M	M	M	M	H	M	L	M

6. LEADERSHIP
   6.1 Policies   L
   6.2 Systems   M
   6.3 Management   M

H = High; consistent evidence/good practice
M = Medium; some evidence/marginal practice
L = Low; no evidence/poor practice

CONCLUSION

The audit offers a practical, economical, and efficient way to conduct a summative assessment of an HRD department, function, or group of interventions. Often it is a good place to start in the journey toward assessing results because it is a familiar process for most organizations. With the right expert doing the audit, it can offer significant opportunities to improve HRD processes and departments.

KEY POINTS TO REMEMBER

▼

- An audit compares actual practices against internal or benchmark standards.
- Audits require a subject matter expert and auditing standards.
- Audits provide an efficient and effective means of gaining an overall assessment of a department, function, or group of interventions.
- An HRD audit framework would key off the five phases of the HRD process: analyze, propose, create, implement, and assess.

Certification
of Core Expertise

Assessment Problem: How do I certify individuals as
having the expertise expected or required of a core
work process? In addition, how do I certify expertise
that is rooted in work processes rather than job duties?

▼

Organizations and consumers of human expertise want to know that individuals have the expertise required by the situation. Chapter Eight provided basic information on assessing knowledge and expertise. This chapter extends that thinking by using knowledge and expertise results to certify employees as having attained necessary levels of expertise to perform well. This is often done when lives could be lost (such as airline pilots), in dangerous occupations (such as chemical plants), or in highly specialized tasks (such as certified public accountant). In fact, it should be considered for all core business processes.

Workplace expertise is the fuel of an organization. Herling (in press) characterizes human expertise as a complex and multifaceted phenomenon and defines it in this way: "Displayed behavior within a specialized domain and/or related domain in the form of consistently demonstrated actions of an individual which are both optimally efficient in their execution and effective in their results." Meeting and maintaining workforce expertise requirements that are connected to organization goals and core work process requirements are a fundamental challenge to organizations. Certifying that expertise requires a new approach that goes beyond the traditional job and task analysis view of expertise to a contemporary business performance improvement model having the following facets: a business goal, a performance requirement, a work process, a process-referenced task analysis, expertise training and development, expertise certification, and performance improvement.

TRADITIONAL JOB-TASK APPROACH TO EXPERTISE

Organizations for the most part have embraced the job- and task-oriented approaches to defining workplace expertise and have relied on multiple analysis procedures (Holton, 1995; Swanson, 1996).

These approaches are familiar to most human resource management professionals and are driven by federal law in many cases. Essentially they all contain three basic steps:

1. Development of a list of job tasks that may be performed in a job
2. Verification of the task list as a valid representation of the job
3. Analysis of precisely what a person needs to know and do to meet a specified performance standard for each task

Fundamentally, job and task analysis methodologies address the proper unit of analysis: the work task. In practice, the custom is often to use existing job structures, current work practices, and current employees as the frame with which to determine the work task requirements. The outcome is task and expertise analyses and certification that are grounded in the present. In stable environments, this approach works. What happens, however, if jobs, work tasks, and task expertise are not stable but changing rapidly, as they are today?

Competency assessment has been developed to overcome some of the limitations of traditional job analysis (DuBois, 1993). Competencies are generally defined as some underlying characteristic of an employee that enables the person to perform the job or task. Because it is an underlying characteristic and one step removed from the tasks themselves, it is a flexible approach that can be used to select and develop employees across multiple jobs.

Competency models generally proceed in the same fundamental steps as the job analysis model, the only difference being that work tasks are analyzed for underlying competencies rather than required knowledge and expertise. In some cases, steps 1 and 2 are skipped and experts are used to develop the competencies directly. The key point is that competency models are also job based; they operate under the same assumptions and are subject to the same criticisms that job-based methods are. To the extent that competencies are more likely than job tasks to be stable, they are an improvement, but they still fall short for all situations, particularly when defining the specific expertise (not general competencies) required to perform.

STRATEGIC APPROACH TO EXPERTISE

What is needed is a new system for identifying and certifying expertise for work outputs that has the following characteristics:

- It is anchored in more stable components of the organization.
- It is flexible as it relates to job structures.
- It separates work expertise and individuals from job structures.
- It addresses organizational, process, and individual levels of performance that can be used strategically, not reactively.

This strategic management of expertise (Swanson and Holton, 1998) is fundamentally different from traditional approaches because it addresses these objectives. In this model, organizations manage strategic goals, core processes, and core competencies and expertise. Employee development systems are focused on expertise, not jobs. Job structures emerge as a final step in the process, but have no real role in the planning. That is, jobs can be reorganized without affecting the planning for expertise. Jobs are expected to change frequently as expertise is redeployed to achieve strategic goals. It is an integrated planning process that links expertise to core business processes, which in turn are linked to customer needs (see Figure 13.1).

This planning process has many implications, but for results assessment purposes, our interest is in how it can lead to more effective identification of expertise needed to achieve organizational goals and how it can be used to develop standards to assess and certify employee expertise.

The basic premise of this approach is that expertise should not be linked to jobs, which are inherently unstable, but to core business

Figure 13.1. Strategic Management of Expertise Flowchart

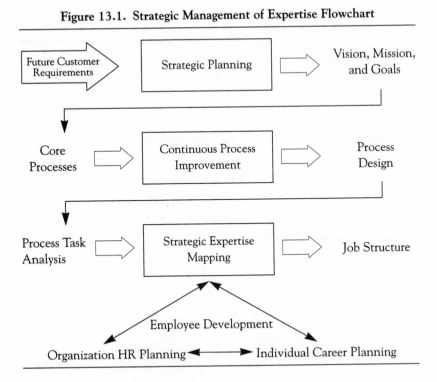

processes for accomplishing organizational goals. Results assessment then takes on a strategic role by certifying core expertise. By linking expertise to business processes instead of jobs, organizations have these characteristics:

- A more flexible expertise structure that allows jobs to be reorganized to encompass different process tasks without requiring new job analysis
- Expertise that is more focused on organizational goals
- A certification system built on process functions rather than positions
- Expertise that is clearly linked to organizational processes

The following case describes how the approach works.

HEALTHCARE INSURANCE INC. CASE

Healthcare Insurance Inc. is facing a serious business problem. Although the company sales force is made up of some extraordinarily capable people, the largest accounts increasingly are being captured by the competition. Sales are down, and analysis has revealed the need to revise the core sales process and the way people do their jobs. Revising the way the work is done ends up putting people working in nine different jobs as contributors to the completion of a sales transaction and also putting them into a new working relationship. Furthermore, the top employees now working in sales do not like the pending changes and are considering leaving. For management the question is, "How can an organization maintain and develop our core workforce expertise in the middle of change?"

The company is a major health care insurance company and provider in the United States. The top executives realized the company's sales process, a core work process, needed revision and realignment in relation to the business goal and the required workforce expertise. Thus, the business goal was focused on increasing sales in a changing and competitive environment. This case clearly illustrates the need for new approaches to building and certifying workplace expertise in fast-changing competitive environments.

Diagnose the Performance

The need for this total effort was fully clarified in a thorough performance improvement proposal based on a rigorous analysis method. Data related to the strategic business goals of Healthcare Inc. were used as a basis for uncovering existing system sales performance problems and solutions. A major conclusion was that the sales process was incapable of meeting the goals of timeliness and quality features necessary to retain market share. Thus, the sales process needed to be significantly improved, the roles in the process needed to be clarified, and the expertise required to carry out the roles within the process needed to be in place.

Document the Existing Process

The existing sales process was documented and found to be a seventy-nine-step process spread over nine job categories. The resulting integrated flowchart, an integration of the steps within the process and the people who work in the process, brings the process and the people working in the process to the fore. In Figure 13.2, each step from the integrated flowchart is coded against all those job roles directly involved in that step. For example, there are three job roles in step 31. Of those, the new business manager (NBM) is primarily responsible for the oversight of this step, with input from case manager (CM) and proposal secretary (Pro). (The bold "X" against the NBM role for step 31 indicates responsibility.) A separate time-sensitive longitudinal flowchart of each of the seventy-nine steps was also produced.

The existing sales process was documented using the following core method:

1. Meet with a select group of salespeople, sales managers, and sales support personnel, and verify and expand on a previously drawn-up job sales task list. In this case interviewees came from four regions throughout the United States.
2. Create a first draft of the integrated flowchart.
3. Visit multiple sales offices, and observe sales personnel and sales support personnel carrying out their work (including going on sales calls).
4. Create a second draft of the integrated flowchart.
5. Send out the sales-integrated flowchart to the select group for review, revision, and approval.

Figure 13.2. Partial List of Sales Process Steps in Relation to Nine Sales-Related Jobs

Jobs and Their Roles in the Process

Implementation & Account Management Subprocess	1. MGMT	2. NBM	3. PSS	4. CM	5. BSC/ Serv	6. Pro	7. UW	8. IM/IS	9. C
25 Assign service representative to case or	X	x							
26 Request case manager from BSC for the case	X				x				
27 Are customer's expectations in sync w/_____ capability to deliver product, price, and service? (If no, go to 15 and 16)				x	x	x	x		x
A **Process Measure:** Number of times _____ capability is not in sync with customer's requirements of cost, product, or service.	X								
28 If yes, review presale file, proposal, and underwriting rates.		x	x	x					
29 Confirm internally what products were sold.		x	x	x	x		x	x	
30+ Advise customer of network developments and/or introduce any new service delivery.		x		x		x			

Jobs and Their Roles in the Process

Implementation & Account Management Subprocess	1. MGMT	2. NBM	3. PSS	4. CM	5. BSC/ Serv	6. Pro	7. UW	8. IM/IS	9. C
31 Notify implementation team of sale and engage.		**X**		x				x	C
•32 **Conduct implementation meeting.** (*Comment:* for management training, stress minor role of NBM)		x		x	x	x		**X**	x
32.1 Answer benefits questions.				x	x			**X**	
32.2 Answer questions on administrative process.				x	x			**X**	
33 Send letter to customer following up on implementation process.				**X**	x			x	
•34+ **Deliver and negotiate financial contracts.**				**X**					x
35 Monitor service process.	x		x	**X**					

X Bold means leadership responsibility, non-bold means contributor.

• **Large, multistep activity**

+ This activity could occur anytime from this point on.

A This step should be automated.

Improve the Process

The integrated flowchart of how the work is done was used as a basis for selecting a group of personnel to review and revise the core sales process. This was done in a face-to-face two-day work session. Each participant had the integrated flowchart prior to the meeting and was informed of the process improvement goal. As each step was reviewed, along with the job roles contributing to that step, improvement revisions were entertained, evaluated, and acted on by the group. In this case, the seventy-nine-step process was reduced to fifty-two steps, and all nine job categories contributing to the existing process continued to contribute to the revised process in a modified manner. In addition, the fifty-two steps were clustered into subprocesses or phases: (1) presale (twenty-four steps), implementation and account management (twenty-five steps), sales renewals (eighteen steps), and settlement (twelve steps). Following the two-day work session, the revised integrated flowchart was sent to a discrete list of organization decision makers for their final approval.

Specify Process-Referenced Tasks

This phase and the next two were completed in one two-day work session. This phase involved the earlier team of experts—the select group of salespeople, sales managers, and sales support personnel— along with the professional trainers, who up to then had been responsible for developing sales expertise in sales personnel and who would be partially responsible for the new sales personnel development system.

Given the improved sales process, the team clustered fifty-two sales process steps into tasks attributable to one or more of the nine job roles in the process. In some instances a single step was equivalent to a task, and in most instances several highly related steps were clustered into a process-referenced task. When this occurred, a task name was given to the grouping of steps. Figure 13.3 visually illustrates this three-step process of producing an integrated flowchart of an existing process, improving the process, and then grouping process steps within job roles into process-referenced job tasks. This phase is relatively easy to do and yet is fundamental in connecting of work tasks to core work processes, something regularly missing in organizations and a source of major performance disconnects in organizations.

Establish Process-Referenced Task Standards (Performance, Knowledge, and Expertise)

This phase can be quite intense. Task standards for each task, in the forms of performance "measure and standard," the "must know" knowledge, and the "must do" expertise, are established. The data sheet shown in Figure 13.4 is used to record decisions.

One critical timesaving aspect to this effort for development purposes is to identify existing documentation and sources of knowledge, expertise, and performance measurement. In fact, invited experts participating in this process were asked to bring along all readily available relevant documentation to the process-referenced tasks under consideration for review and consideration during the work session. In fact, so many good ideas came out so fast from the group that it was critical to have an official recorder of information so that no information was lost.

This highly charged session yielded critical basic information on performance standards, basic knowledge, and unexpected sources of expertise and related training materials. Two of the sales personnel produced such exceptional proposals that the team requested copies from them to use as core training aides.

Produce Task Training and Certification Modules

Following the establishment of process-referenced task standards, the training professionals put together field-based learning modules for those working in the sales process. The learning objectives, field

Figure 13.3. **Three Phases of Specifying Process-Referenced Tasks**

Phase 1: *Integrated Flowchart of a Major Business Procedure As It Is Now (22 process step example)*

Jobs	1	2	3	4	5	6	7	8	9	10	11	12	13	14	15	16	17	18	19	20	21	22
— 1.	x		x		x		x					x					x	x				
— 2.		x	x						x		x	x			x	x						
— 3.	x	x		x				x		x			x			x	x	x	x		x	
— 4.		x	x	x	x	x													x			
— 5.	x			x	x	x		x		x						x	x	x			x	
— 6.				x	x	x			x		x			x	x			x	x	x		x

(Process Activities Over Time)

Phase 2: Improved Integrated Flowchart of a Major Business Procedure As It Will Be (reduced from 22 to 19 steps)

Jobs	1	2	3	4	5	6	7	8	9	10	11	12	13	14	15	16	17	18	19
— 1.	x		x		x		x				x					x	x		
— 2.									x		x			x	x	x		x	x
— 3.	x			x				x		x		x			x	x	x	x	
— 4.		x	x	x	x	x													
— 5.				x	x	x		x		x	x				x	x	x		
— 6.				x		x			x				x	x			x	x	x

(Process Activities Over Time)

Task 1 Task 2 Task 3 Task 4 Task 5

Phase 3:
Process-Referenced Tasks
(e.g., tasks for Job 5)

Figure 13.4. Data Sheet for Establishing Process-Referenced Task Performance, Knowledge, and Expertise Standards

Task #   Take from integrated flowchart

Task Name
- Unique and discrete
- Intermediate and reasonable size
- Action verb and object of action

	Task Knowledge (Must Know)	**Task Expertise** (Must Do)	
Content	If already exists: Name (precisely the document and pages If doesn't exist: List or outline the content	Describe the individual worker's job task work performance (in terms of behaviors, process, and/or outcomes)	*Note: In many instances, these three can be almost alike.*
Measure	If already exists: Name (precisely) the document and pages If doesn't exist: Describe the knowledge (custom-made measure? source for possible measure? paper & pencil? other?)	If already exists: Name (precisely) the document and pages If doesn't exist: Describe the measure	

Performance Measure and Standard
What a worker must do, under what conditions, and to what level

learning guides, and support materials were produced to develop the required knowledge and expertise for sales process-referenced tasks.

In addition, tests were developed and administered to certify knowledge and expertise on a task-by-task basis. Individuals working in the improved sales process were required to be certified in each processed-referenced task within their job. To this end, the personnel certification and development process is illustrated in Figure 13.5.

Case Summary

The strategic management of expertise at Healthcare Inc. proved to be efficient and effective. A significant portion of the activity focused on uncharted territory for the company and the company consultants. Although the individual elements appeared rational and at times routine, the overall perspective of directly connecting business goals and the expertise of individuals was radical. In addition, the time line of eight months to accomplish this with credibility was almost revolutionary.

MANAGING THE DEVELOPMENT OF EXPERTISE

This system points to a fundamentally different approach to developing employees and certifying expertise. Employee development is focused on employees' building a portfolio of certified expertise linked to core processes. A strategic expertise map allows organizations to manage expertise rather than jobs. Employee development systems become future oriented and closely linked to core business processes and critical strategic goals. Employees can manage their careers based on expertise rather than jobs. Jobs, in fact, become temporary holding places that can and will change frequently.

Employees should be selected for both the expertise they bring with them and their capacity to develop new expertise as needs change. Especially in high-technology arenas, expertise may well become obsolete in a short time. In the midst of change, the capacity

Figure 13.5. Personnel Certification and Development Process

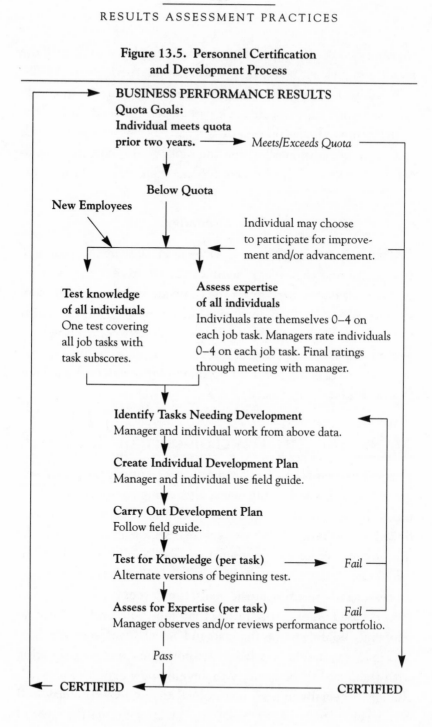

to develop is just as important as current expertise. At Healthcare Inc., sales employees were afraid of the change, in part because their capacity to develop was not adequately considered when they were selected. When their expertise became outdated, they struggled to change.

Organizations should be partners with individuals to determine the expertise and development that will be needed in the future. The organization clearly has the most strategic view and needs to be sure that development will lead to business performance. On the other hand, the individual employee is often the first to realize that changes are occurring in the marketplace and will require new expertise. In many instances, employees recognize the need for new business practices and innovations before management does. Healthcare Inc. could have benefited from a stronger partnership with employees to recognize the need to reengineer sales processes to meet growing competition. As it was, the changes occurred only when competitive pressure reached crisis levels.

RESULTS ASSESSMENT AS CERTIFICATION

The strategic management of expertise brings together several themes in this book to create a certification system to improve organizational performance. By linking a new process of front-end analysis to the knowledge and expertise assessment techniques described in Chapter Eight, an effective expertise certification system can be created. The power of this system is that it starts with organizational performance, not jobs or subject matter, to define expertise and knowledge requirements. Learning domain results assessment is therefore transformed into a powerful process for certifying expertise to perform core organizational processes.

In some instances, it may be appropriate to create formal certification programs, with formal curricula, record keeping, and perhaps designations (such as certified job titles). In these instances, employees may not be allowed to perform certain tasks until they are certified. In other instances, certification may be slightly less formal. We contend that organizations can ill afford to allow the development of core expertise to be poorly operationalized. The strategic management of expertise is limited in scope to core processes having high impact. It can easily be used to certify that employees have the skills they need to achieve organizational goals.

KEY POINTS TO REMEMBER

▼

- The strategic management of expertise through core processes effectively links organizational goals to essential learning and performance.
- Traditional approaches to defining expertise requirements have less application in today's competitive environment.
- Process steps within a core organizational process and the expertise required of the steps ensure workplace relevance.
- When tasks and their required expertise are linked to core processes, impact and flexibility are increased.
- Assessment and certification of expertise certification is a significant role for HRD.

14

CHAPTER

Assessing Performance Drivers

The Learning Organization, Quality Improvement, and Management Development

Assessment Problem: How do I assess results for interventions that are critical to performance but take a long time to produce results or have outcomes that are difficult to predict?

▼

So far we have looked at performance mostly as specific system outcomes, such as services performed or goods produced, and we have emphasized that every intervention should lead to performance outcomes at some point. What we have not discussed fully are those situations where the near-term results of an intervention are not system outcomes but some other intermediate result that will lead to system outcomes in the future—for example:

- Learning organization interventions that are intended to enhance intellectual capital, which in turn is expected to result in increased future performance
- Quality interventions that focus on applying methods for improving work processes
- Management development programs that prepare managers for future leadership roles

In these examples, it would be difficult to identify improvements in system outcomes within the time frame of thirty to ninety days that many organizations would like to hear about results. Yet the interventions could be crucial to strengthening performance over time. A common criticism of results or performance-oriented approaches to developing human resources is that they seem to devalue interventions that do not produce immediate system outcomes. Nothing could be further from the truth.

This chapter shows how the Results Assessment System is applied to this type of intervention, which we have called performance drivers. The Results Assessment System already focuses on a primary performance driver: learning. In many instances, learning directly affects system outcomes by enabling people to do something they could not previously do. In this chapter we explain how to deal with other situations where the effect of the driver on system outcomes is not as direct or occurs over an extended time.

BRIEF REVIEW OF DRIVERS

Recall the two categories of system results: performance outcomes— measures of effectiveness or efficiency relative to core outputs of the system, subsystem, process, or individual—and performance drivers— measures of elements of performance that are expected to sustain or increase system, subsystem, process, or individual ability and capacity to be more effective or efficient in the future (Holton, 1999). Fundamentally, all HRD interventions operate on drivers. Together with outcome measures, drivers describe the hypothesized cause-and-effect relationships in an organization's strategy (Kaplan and Norton, 1996). Thus, drivers should predict future outcomes.

Drivers are vital to organizational success. In fact, most performance improvement interventions—for example, increasing management expertise, new technology, enhancing product quality, improving processes, and increasing employee suggestion—focus on some type of driver. What all these have in common is that they may be vital to maintaining or enhancing system outcomes in the future.

HOW DRIVERS AFFECT
RESULTS ASSESSMENT IN THE SHORT TERM

In skills training, such as the sales communication training case, results assessment is easier than for other types of training. Up-front analysis revealed a relationship between the expertise of the salesperson and sales success. Based on careful analysis, it was determined that the effect of increased communication expertise would have a fairly direct link to increased sales. The outcome would be a results assessment that first looked like this:

Communication expertise → *Increased sales*

In reality, motivating the sales force to use the new expertise required working through the following pattern of effects:

Communication expertise → *System design* → *Rewards* → *Increased sales*

The first situation had several characteristics that made it more straightforward to assess results:

- The relationship was clearly defined. Because of the up-front analysis, the relationship was known with some certainty.
- The link was direct. The learning intervention was expected to have almost a direct effect on the outcomes.
- Outcomes occurred soon after learning. Sales increases were expected to occur quickly after the learning.
- There were few intervening variables. With short time lines, there was less chance for other unplanned factors to influence the outcomes.
- The scope was narrow. This case was confined to one group of employees and a specific realm of expertise.

Many contemporary interventions that focus on drivers, such as the learning organization, quality, and management development, are more complicated or longer term, making results assessment more involved. The learning organization is a popular organization development initiative. Advocates of this strategy suggest that organizations can improve long-term effectiveness by concentrating on creating an organizational system that maximizes learning at the individual, team, and organizational levels (Marquardt, 1996; Senge, 1990; Watkins and Marsick, 1993). Learning organizations have these key characteristics: individuals and teams that work toward the attainment of linked and shared goals; open communication, with information available and shared; systems thinking as the norm;

leaders as champions of learning; management support of learning; an atmosphere that encourages and rewards learning; and a welcoming of new ideas.

In contrast to the simpler example:

- Effect relationships are not clearly defined. The effects are not known with certainty, primarily because it is a relatively new intervention with only anecdotal, not proved, potential.
- The effects occur over many steps. Interventions to create the learning organization are complex, and they fundamentally change many aspects of an organization.
- Outcomes do not occur soon after learning. Interventions to create the learning organization may not produce significant returns for some period of time; perhaps the full effects on outcomes will not be known for several years.
- There are many intervening variables. Because of the three previous characteristics, there is lots of opportunity for other factors—for example, changes in the environment, leadership changes, reorganization—to influence outcomes.
- The scope is wide. Interventions touch all employees and embrace a huge set of competencies.

Clearly, different results assessment strategies are needed to provide assessment in the short term.

A GENERAL FRAMEWORK FOR DRIVER RESULTS ASSESSMENTS

Some people conclude that it is too difficult and complex to assess results for driver interventions. They are wrong. In fact, it is that type of thinking that limits the strategic effectiveness of HRD in organizations. Organizations value only interventions that ultimately lead to true performance outcomes. Many HRD professionals consistently confuse driver outcomes and performance outcomes, thereby losing credibility with decision makers.

It turns out that measures of driver results assessment differ from results assessments in only two basic ways:

1. Performance results are not as predictable. Depending on the intervention, the organization may not know exactly where or how performance results will appear.
2. Performance results may not appear for some period of time. Complete results may not appear for months, or even years.

Figure 14.1 shows these two dimensions in a matrix.

Four types of results assessments emerge. Table 14.1 describes them, along with the adjustments needed in results assessment strat-

Figure 14.1. Performance Driver Matrix

Predictability of Performance Results

		Low	High
Time Until Performance Results Appear	Low	Type 3 Driver Results Assessment	Basic Results Assessment (Sales Communication Case)
	High	Type 2 Driver Results Assessment	Type 1 Driver Results Assessment

Note: The definitions of driver types are given in Table 14.1.

egy. As the table shows, only modest adjustments are needed to make the Results Assessment System work for driver results as well as outcomes.

Type 1 Drivers: The Pattern of Effects

Type 1 drivers, such as management development programs, are the easiest ones to assess. For these drivers, time is the only problem until results occur. Consider how a typical management development program might lead to performance outcomes. Managers attend a series of programs, followed by some period of changing their management

Table 14.1. Performance Driver Assessment Types and Strategies

Type	Description and Example	Steps to Modify Standard Results Assessment Methods
Basic: *High predictability, low time until results*	Classic results assessment case such as the sales communication case discussed in this book	None—use standard approach
Type 1: *High predictability, high time until results*	Interventions with fairly predictable steps to performance, but that take a longer period of time to unfold (e.g., management development)	• Define *pattern of effects* • Use "Performance" row of Results Assessment Plan to identify intermediate results • Measure results at each step until performance is achieved
Type 2: *Low predictability, high time until results*	Interventions where performance results may appear in many different ways and that take a longer period of time to unfold (e.g., learning organization)	• Use Critical Outcome Technique • Repeat at regular intervals • Identify driver results and outcomes
Type 3: *Low predictability, low time until results*	Interventions where performance results may appear in many different ways but are likely to occur within a reasonable time period for assessment (e.g., quality programs)	• Use Critical Outcome Technique • Identify outcomes

practices. Employees notice the change and, after some period of time, trust the changes and become more motivated. Increased motivation might result in increased productivity, which leads to increased sales.

This can be called the *pattern of effects*. Defining this pattern of effects is the key to successful type 1 driver results assessment because the pattern of effects defines the expected relationship between drivers and system outcomes, and intermediate results are expected to occur.

It is quite common for the pattern to be defined incorrectly, as has been the case when trainers assume that people who enjoy training learn more and perform better. Thus, it is essential that the pattern of effects be defined or estimated correctly. In our example, the pattern of effects looks like this:

Manager learning → *Changed manager behavior* →
Employee motivation → *Productivity* → *Sales*

At each step, some result can be measured. That is, at step 1 changes in manager behavior would be assessed. At step 2 changes in employee motivation would be assessed. At step 3 productivity could be assessed, and finally sales would be assessed. It is only the last step, sales, that ultimately justifies the program. All the rest are intermediate outcomes that have value to the organization only because they lead to increased sales.

In the Results Assessment Plan, each of these results would be entered in the system outcomes line (row A) and the word *driver* circled to remind users that the results being assessed were not real outcomes.

Type 2 and Type 3 Drivers

Types 2 and 3 driver results are the hardest to assess. In both cases, the results appear in unpredictable places in the organization. Results assessors literally may not know where to look to measure results, because the results could appear in so many different ways.

The Critical Outcome Technique (COT), introduced in Chapter Eleven, was presented largely as a fill-in strategy to use when a complete analysis had not been conducted. It turns out that the COT is a powerful tool for driver results assessment because it makes no presumption that the outcomes are known in advance—which is exactly the case with type 2 and type 3 drivers.

Type 2 driver results are the most unpredictable and take a long time for results to occur. The learning organization is a classic example. The literature on the learning organization has not been clear on how the expected increases in learning (at multiple levels) will lead to increases in organizational performance and outcomes. The missing link was innovation, as shown in the model in Figure 14.2 (Kaiser and Holton, 1998). A broader look at the literature suggested that changing the organization to have characteristics of a learning organization strategy should lead to increases in learning (driver), which in turn is expected to increase innovation and competitive advantage (drivers). Improved organizational performance results in the form of new or improved goods and services along with financial returns, given an environment of high uncertainty and change.

The problem is that there is little clarity beyond this general scheme. That is, an organization will have no idea exactly what types of learning will occur, what types of innovations could occur, and how they will pay off. Innovations could be anything from product innovations, to work process changes, to research innovations— or all of these.

Unfortunately, many presume that results cannot be assessed because of the unpredictability. In fact, results assessment is still possible, and it is even more important. The following steps are recommended, with time frames modified to suit individual situations:

Figure 14.2. The Learning Organization as a Performance Improvement Strategy

Organization
Characteristics

Learning
Performance
Drivers

Strategic
Performance
Drivers

Performance
Outcomes

Learning
Organization
Strategy

Learning
Outcomes:
– Organizational
– Team
– Individual

Strategic
Outcomes:
– Innovation
– Competitive
  Advantage

Performance
Outcomes:
– New/Improved
  Goods and Services
– Financial Results

1. Set a periodic timetable for results assessment. We suggest every six to nine months.
2. Use the Critical Outcome Technique.
3. Assess critical outcomes in each area where effects are possible or expected.
4. Look at the relationship between results across time periods.

From Figure 14.2, we can see that there are four potential sets of results that could be assessed:

- Implementation of learning organization characteristics
- Learning at the individual, team, and organizational levels
- Innovations and competitive advantage produced
- Organizational performance: new or improved goods and services and financial results

We could measure results at each step, and probably would need to because it could take years for the full benefits of the learning organization to be seen. If the results are plotted over time, we should see a lag effect, where the characteristics start to increase first, followed by learning, followed by innovations, and then by performance outcomes.

Type 3 driver results are a simpler case of type 2. The results are still less predictable, but they tend to occur more quickly. One example might be quality improvement training (quality programs might also be type 3 in some cases). For example, in a state government department of revenue, an outcome measure might be percentage of tax returns processed correctly within two weeks of receipt. A performance driver for that outcome might be the number of quality improvement initiatives successfully implemented as a result of quality improvement teams formed.

The results assessment dilemma here is that the processes that are improved are unknown. Unlike type 3 driver results, though, improvements are expected to occur fairly quickly. Thus, the same procedure is followed as for type 3 drivers, except assessment is conducted only after a reasonable period of time has passed.

GENERAL PRINCIPLES FOR
ASSESSING DRIVER RESULTS

The Results Assessment System embraces both performance outcomes and performance drivers within the realm of system results. This section summarizes principles for assessing results when an intervention is targeted at performance drivers.

Driver results can and should be assessed. All driver interventions produce results, but not all results are outcomes. Some may be intermediate results on the path to outcomes. Thus, all drivers can be assessed, preferably at the driver and outcome stages.

Drivers have no inherent value to the organization, although they may be valuable to the individual or society (learning is an example). Drivers' value comes from the outcomes to which they contribute.

Use the "System" row in the Results Assessment Plan worksheet (Figure 4.1) to plan for driver or outcome results assessment. For assessment of intermediate results, simply circle "driver" on the worksheet, and use the "Performance" row to capture the assessment plan for drivers.

Driver results are often indicator measures of system results. In many instances, the relationship between driver results and system outcomes can be determined and calculated mathematically. For example, we may see that the number of new patents generated is directly related to the number of new products launched in a company and yields certain profits. And we might be able to see historically that the relationship is fairly predictable. Thus, in any given year, the number of patents is a leading indicator of future new products. Another example comes from Reichheld (1996), who has shown that drivers such as customer, employee, and shareholder loyalty are directly related to growth and profits.

Drivers are harder to convert to financial results. The further away from outcomes drivers are in the pattern of effects, the harder they are to convert to dollar results.

Not relating drivers to system and financial results damages credibility. The previous two principles are a seductive trap because they are used as an excuse not to relate drivers to outcomes. Remember, the vast majority of drivers can be related to outcomes, and often to financial results. Intermediate results are not the same as system outcomes, even though some call them "outcomes."

At some point, drivers must be related to system outcomes. Eventually every driver intervention must be perceived as yielding real system outcomes that improve the system's ability to accomplish its mission—for example, profits, lives saved, or taxes collected. Although it is acceptable to assess driver results as an intermediate step, it is not acceptable to rely on driver results forever. Failure to link drivers with outcomes breaks the link with organizational strategy.

In a few instances, it may not be worth the effort to convert drivers to financial results. In some instances drivers are so far removed in time from the outcome results that it is not worth the effort to try to convert them to dollars in the short term. For example, a management development program designed for long-term growth of managers may be so difficult to convert to dollars that it is not worth the effort. Often the end result is an estimate that is so inaccurate that it damages one's credibility.

In the learning organization example, it is okay to measure learning and innovation results (drivers) for a while, but in time those must be shown to improve system performance outcomes, or the intervention should be abandoned. Innovation and learning are not system outcomes. Quality improvement efforts are presumed to lead to greater customer satisfaction and sales. Sales are the system outcomes, and customer satisfaction is an intermediate outcome.

You may have to accept correlational data instead of causal analysis.
Clearly it can be hard to determine that the learning organization
intervention directly causes an increase in competitive advantage
over the span of several years. Because of the many intervening
events, it would be virtually impossible to know that there is a direct
causal relationship. This is true of many driver-type interventions,
particularly those whose benefits take a long time to be realized.

In these cases, correlational data will have to suffice. For example, we cannot be sure that a new "lessons learned" information-
sharing system in a learning organization directly led to more
innovations, a portion of which were turned into new products. But
we may be able to see that as use of that system increased, more new
innovations were reported and more patents applied for.

PREDICTING SYSTEM OUTCOMES
FROM DRIVER RESULTS

Often it is not acceptable to wait for actual system outcomes to occur
before producing system outcome results assessment data and converting the information to financial returns. In those cases, it is desirable to find ways to provide estimates of the likely payoff. The basic
strategy is to find some way to calculate a formula by which driver
results can be converted to likely system outcomes. Here are some
commonly used techniques:

- History. If the organization has had experience with a similar
  type of intervention, calculate the outcomes that occurred from
  them. For example, ABC Company, which is trying a learning
  organization strategy, has applied for patents before and knows
  that it has been successful at converting 20 percent of patents
  into marketable products.
- Industry standards. Frequently industry trade groups maintain
  statistics about the payoff from an intervention. For example,

most industrial groups know that every dollar invested in safety programs is likely to result in a certain percentage reduction in accident costs.

- Benchmarking. When competitive advantage is not at stake, it may be possible to consult similar other organizations to see what their experience has been. For example, a government department could benchmark with other similar government departments to estimate the extent to which quality improvement training is likely to result in improved services to citizens.

- Trend lines. If an organization is in the middle of a multiyear intervention (such as quality or the learning organization), there may already be a partial track record. A trend line could be plotted looking at the increase in performance outcomes from previous steps in the intervention. Quality programs in particular lend themselves to this type of analysis.

- Outside and inside experts. Often outside experts know general formulas to predict outcomes from investments in performance drivers. Inside experts have more intimate knowledge of cost-benefit relationships.

- Consensus estimates. When none of the above data are available, the next best option is to use the consensus estimates from a group of subject matter experts.

CONCLUSION

Assessing results for performance drivers often appears to be difficult, and sometimes nearly impossible. The problem comes from not understanding the difference between driver outcomes and system outcomes. Once properly defined, results assessment strategies are not any more difficult than other assessments and offer useful decision-making data at multiple steps in the process.

KEY POINTS TO REMEMBER

▼

- Results assessment does not have to turn an organization's attention to only human resource interventions that produce short-term outcomes.
- The development of strong, competitive, growing companies requires an intense focus on developing and assessing drivers of performance.
- Defining the performance driver relationships makes results assessment work and provides some discipline to decisions made about driver interventions.

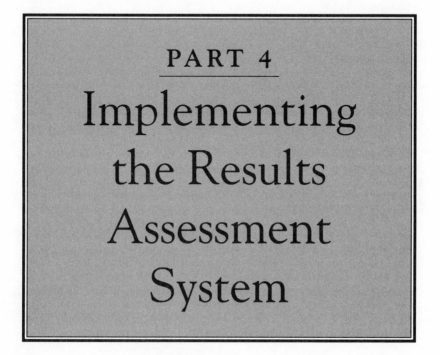

PART 4

Implementing
the Results
Assessment
System

15

Plotting the Journey to Results Assessment

Assessment Problem: How do I make results assessment an integral and continuous part of the human resource development process?

▼

Results assessment is not a routine component of most HRD practice. Organization development and personnel training and development programs are often implemented with little or no formal plans for assessment or no thoughts regarding follow-up procedures designed to identify measurable outcomes. Because conducting such assessments is not standard within HRD practice, most organizations do not have the expertise, culture, or systems in place to make it easy to implement. So far, this book has focused mostly on building your knowledge and expertise in results assessment. In this chapter we turn to eight key strategies for overcoming common organizational culture and systems issues that professionals confront as they work to implement results assessment.

WHAT HAPPENS AFTER YEARS WITHOUT RESULTS ASSESSMENT

To illustrate the effects of neglecting results assessment, let us pay a visit to the HRD group of XYZ Company to examine its results assessment process. This HRD group of internal organization development consultants, like most others, has never been asked to assess outcomes beyond participant or stakeholder perceptions. All too often results remain unidentified and unmeasured. For example, extensive efforts to build effective self-directed work teams have been assessed only using worker satisfaction measures. Accordingly, there is often a tremendous gap between the programs and the outcomes they are designed to generate. By neglecting the outcomes, the XYZ organization unknowingly fosters a climate that seems largely indifferent to producing measurable outcomes.

In XYZ and similar other companies, managers and members of the HRD group are happy to report their performance in terms of reaction data, departments served, programs offered, and so forth. Although this information may be invaluable in terms of cost and feasibility analyses, it says nothing about the change that has occurred, performance improvements, or the value that the HRD program has added to the company. In short, these reports fail to capture the essence of the mission and goals of the organization and the specific demands placed on HRD, and they offer no valuable information regarding results.

What has developed in this type of organization is typical of those that have not focused on results and results assessment. Over the years, HRD activities become increasingly isolated from the systems they are designed to support, and HRD professionals and line managers become less and less closely associated. Eventually programs take on a life of their own separate from the goals and work processes to achieve them. A culture of mediocrity, at least as far as learning and performance, takes over. *The solution is to create a culture of results.*

Throughout this book, we have stressed the importance of assessing performance results as well as learning and perceptions. However, results assessment rarely succeeds in assessing performance outcomes, let alone learning, when assessment is only an occasional event. The most effective strategy is to create a culture where results assessments become routine and expected.

The biggest barrier to creating the assessment culture is the widespread "education" mentality that is deeply ingrained in the minds of HRD professionals. The idea that individual development is supposed to lead to something afterward (such as organizational performance in the case of learning in organizations) is very much a foreign concept. HRD professionals must break out of this mold and readjust their thinking to focus on results that substantially advance the mission and goals of their host organization. This is not an easy task. The performance culture is radically different, it takes time to create, and it brings with it all the problems usually associated with culture change, such as resistance and people who are slow to change.

OVERCOMING RESISTANCE TO RESULTS ASSESSMENT

Let us consider first some strategies to use when introducing results in assessment in organizations or groups where it has not previously occurred. Here are four key strategies for overcoming resistance to change.

Overcoming Resistance Strategy 1: Implement only what the culture will allow

The first hard lesson that results assessment professionals must learn is that many people in organizations do not welcome results assessment. Imagine implementing results assessment in XYZ Company. It is highly unlikely that it would be welcomed and embraced immediately. Most likely, one of these typical reactions from implementing results assessment would occur:

- Fear that the results will not be good
- Anxiety about how the data will be used
- Uncertainty about why results assessment is needed
- Doubt about the validity of assessing results from learning
- Discomfort that the program must lead to organizational and individual performance
- Anger that someone is "checking up" on outcomes
- A wish that self-directed development was sufficient

Ironically, the individuals and companies with the most to gain from results assessment also have the most to lose if the results are not good. Thus, the resistance may be greater in organizations that have the most to gain.

Introducing results assessment into an organization has to be seen as both a measurement task with associated technical issues and a cultural change process. Successful change to a results assessment culture requires that assessors focus equal attention on both the measurement task and the change process.

Overcoming Resistance Strategy 2: Compromise on measurement issues in the early stages to gain acceptance

Insisting on rigorous measurement too soon after introducing results assessment is a common mistake. Conducting more lenient measurement initially and increasing the rigor as the culture adjusts is a preferable approach with a greater likelihood for acceptance. Although the measurement from early efforts will be less accurate, it will also be less threatening. Over time, participants themselves often begin to demand more accurate data, which is exactly what you want them to do.

Measurement, particularly rigorous performance measurement, can be intimidating to people unaccustomed to it. Furthermore, it often requires some effort by those involved in the process to collect and validate the data. Thus, it is easy for managers and participants to sabotage assessment efforts that they perceive as threatening. If initiated too early, rigorous results assessment efforts are almost certain to do that.

The key is to implement what the culture will allow, plus perhaps a little more, and then add to it as acceptance is gained. After a few results assessments are implemented, people usually will see the value of results assessment effort and realize it is not something to fear.

Overcoming Resistance Strategy 3: Sell results assessment

Do not expect everyone to welcome you with open arms when you propose results assessment. Even senior management may need to be sold on the idea of assessing results from HRD activities. Line managers may see it as another demand on their time and may need to be convinced that it will help them in some way. Participants may be afraid that upper management is checking up on them and not realize that they will benefit.

In short, you must be prepared to sell the process to senior management, line management, and participants. Here are some key benefits each group is likely to receive from implementing a program of results assessments; you can use them as selling points:

Selling Points for Senior Management
• Increased productivity as a result of HRD
• Better use of dollars invested in HRD
• More satisfied line management

Selling Points for Line Management
• More immediate payoffs from HRD activities
• Increased productivity
• Greater involvement in HRD goals and planning
• Less time wasted on low-value interventions

Selling Points for Participants
• More accurately targeted HRD interventions
• Clearer goals and performance outcomes
• Less time wasted
• Increased opportunities for feedback about program outcomes

Overcoming Resistance Strategy 4: Provide incentives and rewards for results assessment

You cannot ask people in organizations to do things they fear without providing incentives and rewards. Introducing results assessment in organizations is no different, particularly when it is an optional rather than mandatory activity. Incentives and rewards serve several purposes, including sending clear signals about the importance of results assessment, encouraging participants to take risks, and gaining support from key opinion leaders.

One frequent response to this suggestion is the statement by HRD managers that they do not have any authority to offer incentives and rewards. We disagree. Consider these examples:

- Offer extra assistance to the first groups willing to participate.
- Give preferential access to HRD resources for results assessment participants.
- Develop special interventions to address performance improvement needs.
- Publicly celebrate accomplishments of participating divisions or groups.

Upper management has more power to offer incentives and rewards like these:

- Extra resources to fund results assessment and subsequent interventions
- Higher status to groups using best results assessment practices
- New processes to review and act on results assessment recommendations
- Public support of and emphasis on results assessment

Organizations that are serious about results assessment recognize that incentives and rewards act as important signposts on the journey.

IMPLEMENTING RESULTS ASSESSMENT AS A SYSTEM

After overcoming initial resistance to results assessment, attention turns to how to make it a system. So far we have talked about results assessment mostly as an event, not as part of the larger organizational and HRD systems. Although this is understandable in the early stages of introducing results assessment, it is an ineffective strategy for the long term. For results assessment to succeed in advancing a performance culture, it must become an integral part of the core HRD system. Recall that assessment is the final phase of the five-phase HRD process: analyze, propose, create, implement, and assess. This section offers five key strategies to help integrate results assessment into the organizational system.

Implementation Strategy 1:
Link results assessment to up-front analysis

Results assessment is not a separate HRD process, despite the fact that it requires different tools. It is not uncommon to hear professionals refer to evaluation as if it were a process separate and distinct from the rest of the HRD system. Nothing could be more incorrect. Results assessment is best conceived and implemented as the complementary process to front-end analysis.

In fact, most results assessment "problems" usually turn out to be analysis problems. The reason is that it is within the up-front analysis phase where the knowledge, expertise, and performance outcomes are defined. Practitioners who say they "can't perform results assessment" usually mean the outcomes of the HRD have not been defined clearly enough and the practitioners do not know how to define them in order to conduct a results assessment.

Interestingly, most analysis systems for performance improvement (Swanson, 1996) are conceptually identical to results assessment, but in reverse order. Complete up-front analysis starts at the performance level, identifying what performance issues (problems or goals) need to be addressed. This could be done at the individual, process, and organizational level. Once identified, the performance issues are studied to identify work expertise that is needed or needs to be changed. Finally, the knowledge necessary to develop the expertise is specified.

Results assessment, if all options are chosen, works within the same domains but usually in reverse order. That is, after a learning intervention, knowledge assessment is conducted to assess what is learned; work expertise is assessed to see if the knowledge can be applied; and finally, performance is assessed to see if the performance issues have been addressed.

Implementation Strategy 2:
Embed results in program design

We remember one organization's training director who wanted to try results assessment. She asked that it include pretests of learning as well as performance. Because the program was a series of modules spread over multiple days, multiple instruments were developed and administered during the training. When the plan was presented to the training staff, they were outraged by the "extra time and effort" that would be required. They did not want to do it, in part because of fear, as it later became apparent. The training director ordered it implemented anyway.

A funny thing happened: the trainers loved it! They had not realized how the results assessment process would make their training task easier or how it would make the training more meaningful for the participants. Among the key benefits were these:

- It was clearer to trainees that the organization was serious about this learning.
- Trainees and trainers more clearly understood what outcomes were expected.
- Learning measures became a source of in-process feedback to the trainees, as well as the trainers.
- The test instruments initiated discussions that clarified key learning points.
- Missed test questions became a learning tool for trainers and trainees.

- Trainers modified instructional techniques where needed to improve learning.
- Trainers modified the balance of instructional techniques to focus more on expertise for performance rather than just learning.

The lesson here is clear: the more fully that results assessment becomes integrated with the learning process, the more successful it will be. Unfortunately, the tendency is to treat it as a "research" project, often conducted by an outside expert, which takes place either parallel to or outside the learning process itself. It is not uncommon to see the data disappear with the analysts and the results shared with only a select group of people. This approach almost ensures that results assessment will be resented as an outside intrusion and perhaps ignored.

Implementation Strategy 3:
Create stakeholder ownership of results

Assessment is often something "done to" participants by outside experts. The outcome is often increased resistance and participants who attack the data as invalid simply because they do not own them. Results assessments that work transfer much of the ownership of the results, and the results assessment, to the stakeholders—primarily the participants and their management. As long as results assessment "belongs" to the HRD department, stakeholders have little reason to take it seriously.

In addition, it is frequently the stakeholders who have the best insight into how results should be assessed. When performance results are important, the participants and their management, not the HRD group, will understand them best. The participants can best define the desired outcomes and outcome measures that will work. Thus, it is very difficult for HRD professionals to make results assessment a system without at least sharing ownership of the process and the measures.

Finally, as a practical matter, most HRD departments do not have the staff to manage all the results assessments that are necessary. By placing ownership with stakeholders, HRD staff members are freed up to initiate other projects or assessments. Not only is it a more effective approach, it is a more efficient one as well. Here are some strategies to build stakeholder ownership of results assessment:

- Expect results to occur.
- Involve stakeholders in determining the measures for performance, learning, and perceptions.
- Make participants accountable for successful performance and learning results.
- Make management responsible for collecting, monitoring, and reacting to performance results.
- Make sure all stakeholders receive reports of all results assessment data.
- Have stakeholders validate results data.
- Engage stakeholders in problem solving to correct results that do not conform with standards.
- Have participants and managers conduct as much results assessment as is practical.
- Integrate results assessment into existing assessment systems, such as strategic planning or departmental performance reviews.

Implementation Strategy 4: Use existing measurement and data systems whenever possible

Too often results assessors create their own measurement and data systems to assess results from learning. Occasionally this is necessary, but more often than not it is a waste of effort and resources. Furthermore, these systems are almost certain to fail because most employees are already burdened with more work than they can do within the time available. Adding another process on top of many others does not work.

Effective results assessors look for opportunities to use or build on existing systems. This takes on several forms:

- Use existing data whenever possible before creating new measures. Most organizations already have a wealth of data, particularly performance data, to draw on.
- Integrate results assessment with other organizational performance review processes. Results assessment should become part of regular review processes. For example, assessing work process effectiveness and efficiency should usually be integrated with regular expertise and capacity reviews. Performance improvement from HRD should be part of whatever regular periodic process is used to review the work unit's performance.
- Use existing databases and data collection systems. The more results data can be collected and managed as part of other data collection systems, the greater likelihood that assessment will persist. New data collection systems should be created only after careful deliberation.

Implementation Strategy 5: Make results measurement a learning process in itself

One function of results assessment is clearly to improve accountability for outcomes from HRD interventions. However, if that is all that it is used for, it is not likely to work well.

To be effective, Results Assessment Systems also need to be used as a learning process itself. If working properly, results assessments should reveal potential problem areas, needs for improvement, and changes that can be made to strengthen organizational results. If the primary outcomes of finding areas for improvement are reprimands or other accountability-related actions, people will come to fear results assessment. If these findings are also viewed through a learning lens as a means of continuous improvement and advancement, fear can be minimized.

An organization can learn much about itself by rewarding and celebrating those who find ways to improve effectiveness. Both the quality improvement and learning organization movements have promoted just such an organizational culture. Without some safe space within which people are willing and able to be self-reflective and critical, organizations develop blind spots and are unable to stay competitive.

The challenge is to find the balance. It is clearly not acceptable to allow poor results to persist. HRD investments can be substantial, and outcomes should be demanded. However, this must be balanced with the need to encourage people to learn from mistakes and strive to improve.

KEY POINTS TO REMEMBER
▼

- Implementing results assessment is a journey that must be managed as an organizational change process.

  – Implement what the culture will allow.
  – Compromise on measurement issues to build acceptance.
  – Sell the process.
  – Provide incentives and rewards.

- For long-term effectiveness, results assessment must be a system integrated with other organizational systems.

  – Link it to up-front analysis.
  – Embed results in program design.
  – Create stakeholder ownership.
  – Use existing measurement systems.
  – Make it a learning process.

CHAPTER

16

Getting Started

Assessment Problem: How do I get started on the journey to results assessment?

▼

In Chapter Two the five-step results assessment process was introduced; each chapter of the book has taken one step or aspect of the process and provided the tools to implement the step. Together these tools and process provide an unusual package with the following components:

- A complete system of tools and components in a tightly organized process. Unlike books that provide collections of methods and tools, this book sets out an integrated system we call the Results Assessment System.
- A system and process based on sound theory and research. The Results Assessment System is deeply rooted in the best knowledge we have.
- Results assessment tools that can be implemented by the average HRD practitioner. The Results Assessment System is not so simple that anyone can do it, but a reasonably competent HRD professional or line-manager should be able to use it with appropriate amounts of study.
- A three-domain, six-dimension framework for thinking about results from learning interventions: performance results, with system and financial dimensions; learning results, with knowledge and expertise dimensions; and perception results, with participant and stakeholder dimensions.

OVERCOMING ROADBLOCKS

So what is your thinking right now? Here are some common reactions and our responses to them:

"This is too hard to do in my organization." No, it is not! Reread Chapters Four and Fifteen for ways to start small, and then get better and bigger results assessment.

"My organization may buy it, but I am not sure that I personally can do it." Many HRD professionals are intimidated by results

assessment, so you are not alone. That is why we created a process, tools, and worksheets to guide you. When you follow the process and use the system, you will become more comfortable with it.

"I'm not sure people here are ready to do all domains." Then do not start with all of them. There is a big difference between where you can start and where you should try to end up. It is okay to start with what is practical and then move to the best practice level.

"People here are happy with perception data. Why do I need more?" We have made the case throughout the book that perception data alone are fundamentally flawed as criteria for making HRD decisions. Most HRD practitioners who have settled for perceptions, usually in the form of reaction data, have regretted it when called to justify their department's activities. Do not make the same mistake.

"It looks as if it will take too much time and too many resources to do this." This common concern is valid, but only in the early stages. Like any other change, it consumes extra time and energy at first. But it does not take long before the payoffs from results assessment far exceed the extra effort. Using a careful plan, like that set out in Chapter Four, will end up saving time and resources.

"I am scared of this." Congratulations on your candor. If you have never assessed results from HRD like this before, it can be intimidating. And you will likely find out that some of your programs are not working as well as you would like. But it is far better to fix the problems than to let them linger.

THE PLEASURE OF RESULTS

Our experience is that HRD organizations that take results, and results assessment, seriously find that it brings them considerable pleasure. Here are some of the common reasons:

- Getting results says you have accomplished something. It feels good to make a difference and to help individuals and the organization improve.
- Measuring results gives you concrete evidence of the accomplishment. Instead of just believing, or having faith that what you do helps, you know that you make a difference.
- Results assessment builds confidence. Knowing that you made a difference builds confidence that you can be a major factor in the organization's success.
- Results assessment helps justify your role in the organization. Should you ever have to justify what you do to upper management, you will have concrete evidence of HRD's impact.
- Results build integrity. You can look a manager in the eye and say without a doubt that you can improve performance.
- Getting results gives you more status and importance in the organization. The more you can affect your organization's mission, the more valued you become.

Concluding Point

Imagine that assessing and reporting results from interventions was the rule in the human resource development profession, not the exception to the rule. This would change everything. The ultimate by-product of fully implementing the Results Assessment System is for human resource development to be taken seriously at all levels as an organizational partner dedicated to producing positive results.

References

Alliger, G. M., and Janak, E. A. (1989). "Kirkpatrick's levels of training criteria: Thirty years later." *Personal Psychology, 42,* 331–340.

Alliger, G., Tannenbaum, S. I., Bennett, W., Jr., Traver, H., and Shotland, A. (1997). "A meta-analysis of the relations among training criteria." *Personnel Psychology, 50,* 341–358.

American Heritage college dictionary. (3rd ed.) (1993). Boston: Houghton Mifflin.

Arvey, R. D., and Cole, D. A. (1989). "Evaluating change due to training." In I. L. Goldstein (Ed.), *Training and development in organizations.* San Francisco: Jossey-Bass.

Bassi, L., Benson, G., and Cheney, S. (1996). *Trends: Position yourself for the future.* Alexandria, VA: ASTD Press.

Bassi, L., and Cheney, S. (1996). *Results from the 1996 benchmarking forum.* Alexandria, VA: ASTD Press.

Bassi, L. J., Gallagher, A. L., and Schroer, E. (1996). *The ASTD training data book.* Alexandria, VA: ASTD Press.

Bates, R., Holton, E. F., III, and Seyler, D. (1997). "Factors affecting transfer of training in an industrial setting." In R. Torraco (Ed.), *Proceedings of the 1997 Academy of Human Resource Development Annual Meeting.* Atlanta, GA.

Becker, G. S. (1993). *Human Capital: A theoretical and empirical analysis with special reference to education.* Chicago: University of Chicago Press.

Bereiter, C., and Scardamalia, M. (1993). *Surpassing ourselves: An inquiry into the nature and implications of expertise.* Chicago: Open Court.

Brinkerhoff, R. O. (1995). "Using evaluation to improve the quality of technical training." In L. Kelly (Ed.), *The ASTD technical and skills training handbook*. New York: McGraw-Hill.

Brinkerhoff, R. O. (1997). "Response to: Values as a vital supplement to the use of financial analysis in HRD." *Human Resource Development Quarterly*, 8(1).

Carnevale, B., and Schulz, E. (1990). "Technical training in America: How much and who." *Training and Development Journal*, 42(11), 18–32.

Cronbach. (1982). *Designing evaluations of educational and social programs*. San Francisco: Jossey-Bass.

Davis, J. R., and Davis, A. B. (1998). *Effective training strategies: A comprehensive guide to maximizing learning in organizations*. San Francisco: Berrett-Koehler.

Dean, P. J., and Ripley, D. E. (1997). *Performance improvement pathfinders: Models for organizational learning systems*. Washington, DC: ISPI Press.

Dixon, N. M. (1990). "The relationship between trainee responses on participation reaction forms and posttest scores." *Human Resource Development Quarterly*, 1, 129–137.

Dubois, D. (1993). *Competency-based performance improvement*. Amherst, MA: HRD Press.

Edvinsson, L., and Malone, M. S. (1997). *Intellectual capital: Realizing your company's true value by finding its hidden brainpower*. New York: Harper-Collins.

Fitz-Enz, J. (1994). "Yes . . . you can weigh training's value." *Training*, 7, 54–58.

Gagne, R. M., and Medsker, K. L. (1996). *The conditions of learning: Training applications*. New York: Harcourt Brace.

Goldstein, I. L. (1986). *Training in organizations: Needs assessment, development, and evaluation*. (2nd ed.) Pacific Grove, CA: Brooks/Cole.

Grove, D. A., and Ostroff, C. (1990). "Program evaluation." In K. N. Wexley (Ed.), *Developing human resources*. Washington, DC: BNA.

Herling, R. (in press). "Expertise: The development of an operational definition for human resource development." *Human Resource Development International*.

Holton, E. F., III. (1995). "A snapshot of needs assessment." In J. Phillips and E. F. Holton III (Eds.), *In action: Conducting needs assessment* (pp. 1–12). Alexandria, VA: ASTD Press.

Holton, E. F., III. (1996). "The flawed four-level evaluation model." *Human Resource Development Quarterly*, 7(1), 5–29.

Holton, E. F., III. (1999). "Performance domains and their boundaries." In R. Torraco (Ed.), *Advances in developing human resources: The theory and practice of performance improvement* (Vol. 1). San Francisco: Berrett-Koehler.

Holton, E. F., III, Bates, R. A., Ruona, W.E.A., and Leimbach, M. (1998). "Development and validation of a generalized learning transfer climate questionnaire: Final report." In R. Torraco (Ed.), *Proceedings of the 1998 Academy of Human Resource Development Annual Meeting*, Chicago.

Jacobs, R. L., and Jones, M. J. (1995). *Structured on-the-job training: Unleashing employee expertise in the workplace*. San Francisco: Berrett-Koehler.

Kaiser, S. M., and Holton, E. F., III. (1998). "The learning organization as a performance improvement strategy." In R. Torraco (Ed.), *Proceedings of the 1998 Academy of Human Resource Development Annual Meeting*, Chicago.

Kaplan, R. S., and Norton, D. P. (1996). *The balanced scorecard: Translating strategy into action*. Boston: Harvard Business School Press.

Kirkpatrick, D. L. (1998). *Evaluating training programs: The four levels*. San Francisco: Berrett-Koehler.

Knowles, M. S., Holton, E. F., III, and Swanson, R. A. (1998). *The adult learner*. (5th ed.) Houston: Gulf Publishing.

Krugman, P. (1994). *Peddling prosperity*. New York: Norton.

Kusy, M. (1988). "The effects of types of training evaluation on support of training among corporate managers." *Performance Improvement Quarterly*, 1(2), 23–30.

Marquardt, M. J. (1996). *Building the learning organization*. Alexandria, VA: ASTD Press.

Mattson, B. W. (1999). The development and validation of the critical outcome technique. *Human Resource Development International*, 2(4).

Mattson, B. W., Quartana, L. J., and Swanson, R. A. (1998). "Assessing the business results of management development using the critical outcome technique at CIGNA Corporation." In R. J. Torraco (Ed.), *Academy of Human Resource Development 1998 Annual Proceedings*. Baton Rouge, LA: AHRD.

McLean, G. N. (1988). *Construction and analysis of organization climate surveys*. St. Paul: University of Minnesota HRD Research Center.

268

REFERENCES

Micklewait, J., and Woolridge. A. (1996). *The witch doctors: Making sense of the management gurus*. New York: Random House.

Newstrom, J. (1995). "Review: Evaluating training programs: The four levels." *Human Resource Development Quarterly*, 6(3), 317–320.

Patton, M. Q. (1990). *Qualitative evaluation and research methods*. Thousand Oaks, CA: Sage.

Phillips, J. J. (1996). *Accountability in human resource management*. Houston: Gulf Publishing.

Reichheld, F. F. (1996). *The loyalty effect: The hidden force behind growth, profits, and lasting value*. Boston: Harvard Business School Press.

Robinson, A., and Stern, S. (1997). *Corporate creativity: How innovation and improvement actually happen*. San Francisco: Berrett-Koehler.

Rummler, G. A., and Brache, A. P. (1995). *Improving performance: How to manage the white space on the organization chart*. San Francisco: Jossey-Bass.

Senge, P. M. (1990). *The fifth discipline: The art and practice of the learning organization*. New York: Doubleday Currency.

Sleezer, C. (Ed.). (1989). *Improving human resource development through measurement*. Alexandria, VA: ASTD Press.

Sleezer, C., and Swanson, R. A. (1992). "Culture surveys." *Management Decision*, 30(2), 22–29.

Swanson, R. A. (1989). "Everything important in business and industry is evaluated." In R. O. Brinkerhof (Ed.), *Evaluating training programs in business and industry*. New Directions for Program Evaluation. San Francisco: Jossey-Bass.

Swanson, R. A. (1995). Human resource development: Performance is the key. *Human Resource Development Quarterly*, 6(2), 207–213.

Swanson, R. A. (1996). *Analysis for improving performance: Tools for diagnosing organizations and documenting workplace expertise*. San Francisco: Berrett-Koehler

Swanson, R. A. (1998). Demonstrating the financial benefit of human resource development: Status and update on the theory and practice. *Human Resource Development Quarterly*, 9(3), 285–295.

Swanson, R. A., and Fentress, J. H. (1975). The effect of instructor influential tactics on their evaluation by university students. *Journal of Industrial Teacher Education*, 13(1), 5–16.

Swanson, R. A., and Gradous, D. B. (1988). *Forecasting financial benefits of human resource development*. San Francisco: Jossey-Bass.

Swanson, R. A., and Holton, E. F., III. (1998). "Process-referenced expertise: Developing and maintaining core expertise in the midst of change." *National Productivity Review, 17*(2), 29–38.

Swanson, R. A., and Mattson, B. W. (1997). "Development and validation of the critical outcome technique (COT)." In R. Torraco (Ed.), *Academy of Human Resource Development 1996 Annual Proceedings*.

Swanson, R. A., and Mattson, B. W. (1998). "Electronic support for the performance-learning-satisfaction evaluation system." In P. Dean and D. Ripley (Eds.), *Performance improvement interventions: Performance technologies in the workplace* (pp. 400–420). Washington, DC: ISPI Press.

Swanson, R. A., and Swanson, B. L. (1996). *Audit report of human resource development practices in a large multi-national corporation*. St. Paul: University of Minnesota HRD Research Center.

Tribus, M. (1985). *Becoming competitive by building the quality company*. Kingsport, TN: American Quality and Productivity Institute.

Torraco, R. J., and Swanson, R. A. (1995). "The strategic roles of human resource development." *Human Resource Planning, 18*(4), 10–21.

Torraco, R. A., and Swanson, R. A. (1997). "The strategic audit of HRD as a change intervention." In E. F. Holton III (Ed.), *Leading organizational change*. Alexandria, VA: ASTD Press.

Ulrich, D. (1997). *Human resource champions: The next agenda for adding value and delivering results*. Boston: Harvard Business School Press.

Warr, P., and Bunce, D. (1995). Trainee characteristics and the outcomes of open learning. *Personnel Psychology, 48*, 347–375.

Watkins, K. E., and Marsick, V. J. (1993). *Sculpting the learning organization*. San Francisco: Jossey-Bass.

Index

▼

139–140. *See also* Participant perceptions; Ratings; Stakeholder perceptions

Performance: defined, 16; domain of results, 14, 16

Performance analysis, 171. *See also* Front-end analysis

Performance diagnosis matrix, 72, 73, 171

Performance diagnosis process, 171, 172; applied to learning, 178–184; applied to transfer of learning, 171–184

Performance dimensions: quality, 67, 68–69; quantity, 67, 68; time, 67, 68

Performance driver matrix, 233–234

Performance drivers: correlational data from, 242; defined, 70; general framework for assessment of, 233–240; general principles for assessment of, 240–242; importance of, 71, 231; interim valuing of, 28, 67–68, 69–76, 78, 230, 240–241; key points about, 244; learning as, 230; for learning organization interventions, 70, 75, 230, 232–233, 235, 237, 238, 241, 242; for management development interventions, 70, 230, 235–236; measurement of, 69–76, 229–244; pattern of effects type of, 72–74, 235–236; performance outcomes connection to, 16–17, 27–28, 65, 67–76, 78, 240–241; as performance quality features, 67–69; predicting system outcomes from, 74–75, 230–233, 242–243; for quality interventions, 70, 230, 235, 239–240, 241; and result assessment, 231–233, 234; situations requiring assessment of, 70, 230, 235; Type 1, 72–74, 235–236; Type 2, 235, 236–240; Type 3, 235, 236–240; types of, 235–240

Performance indicator measures, 140–141

Performance levels, performance variables and, 73

Performance results/outcomes, 14, 16–17; categories and dimensions of, 67–69; Critical Outcome Technique for, 189–209; measurement of, 28–29, 59–78, 79–100; options in, 14, 16; performance drivers connection to, 16–17, 27–28, 65, 67–76, 78, 230, 231–233, 240–241; planning expected, 26–28; reporting, 30–31; in sales communication case study, 26–28, 30–31. *See also* Financial results; System results

Performance valuing/worksheet, 82–83, 86–87, 90–91, 92–93

Performance variables, 73, 171; in transfer of learning, 171–177

Periodic cycle sampling, 50

Personal interaction knowledge test, 120

Personnel assessment and development process, 225, 226

Planning. *See* Results Assessment Plan

Practicality: checklist for, 56; importance of, 46; principles of, 46–51

Process improvement, 220, 223

Process measures of expertise, 123–125, 217–219

Process perceptions, 137–140. *See also* Perception results

Process-referenced tasks: certification in, 225, 226; establishing standards for, 221, 224; specification of, 220–221, 222–223

Project Management Certificate Program, 199

Promises, making credible, 51–52

Propose phase of HRD, 10; audit of, 205; cost analysis of, 95

Publishing House case example, 61–63

Purposive samples, 51

Q

Quality dimension to performance, 67, 68–69. *See also* Performance drivers

Quality improvement PDCP (plan-do-check-act) cycle, 13

Quality interventions: perception instrument for, 142, 143–148; performance drivers applied to, 70, 230, 235, 239–240, 241

Quartana, L. J., 196

The Authors

▼

Richard A. Swanson is a professor at the University of Minnesota and a senior partner of Swanson and Associates, Inc., and is an internationally recognized authority on organizational change, performance improvement, and human resource development. He has performed consulting work for several of the largest corporations in the United States and around the world and has conducted study trips to Great Britain, Japan, Germany, Netherlands, and South Africa. He is immediate past president of the Academy of Human Resource Development. In 1993 he received the American Society for Training and Development (ASTD) professor's network national award for his "Outstanding Contribution to the Academic Advancement of Human Resource Development." And in 1995 ASTD/AHRD established the Richard A. Swanson Award for Excellence in Research. Among his more than two hundred publications are *Analysis for Improving Performance* (Berrett-Koehler, 1996), *Human Resource Development Research Handbook: Linking Research and Practice* (Berrett-Koehler, 1997) and *The Adult Learner 5th Edition* (Gulf, 1998). Swanson was the founding editor of the *Human Resource Development Quarterly* and is serving as the founding editor of the *Advances in Developing Human Resources* monograph series.

Elwood F. Holton III is an associate professor of human resource development at Louisiana State University, where he also coordinates and teaches in the HRD degree programs. His research focuses on analysis, design, and evaluation of organizational performance systems. His consulting work takes him frequently to large corporations, government agencies, nonprofit organizations, and universities. He is president of the Academy of Human Resource Development. Holton is the author of over one hundred publications, including academic and professional articles in journals such as *Advances in Developing Human Resources, Human Resource Development Quarterly, Human Resource Development International, Performance Improvement Quarterly, Human Resource Management Review, International Journal of Training and Development, Journal of Organizational and Occupational Psychology, Training and Development,* and the *Journal of Business and Psychology.* Holton's recent books include *The Adult Learner 5th Edition* (Gulf Publishing, 1998); *The Ultimate New Employee Survival Guide* (Peterson's, 1998); *Human Resource Development Research Handbook: Linking Research and Practice* (Berrett-Koehler, 1997); and *Leading Change in Organizations* (ASTD, 1997). He is on the editorial boards of *Human Resource Development Quarterly, Human Resource Development International,* and *Advances in Developing Human Resources.*

Berrett-Koehler Publishers

BERRETT-KOEHLER is an independent publisher of books, periodicals, and other publications at the leading edge of new thinking and innovative practice on work, business, management, leadership, stewardship, career development, human resources, entrepreneurship, and global sustainability.

Since the company's founding in 1992, we have been committed to supporting the movement toward a more enlightened world of work by publishing books, periodicals, and other publications that help us to integrate our values with our work and work lives, and to create more humane and effective organizations.

We have chosen to focus on the areas of work, business, and organizations, because these are central elements in many people's lives today. Furthermore, the work world is going through tumultuous changes, from the decline of job security to the rise of new structures for organizing people and work. We believe that change is needed at all levels—individual, organizational, community, and global—and our publications address each of these levels.

We seek to create new lenses for understanding organizations, to legitimize topics that people care deeply about but that current business orthodoxy censors or considers secondary to bottom-line concerns, and to uncover new meaning, means, and ends for our work and work lives.

See next page for other books from Berrett-Koehler Publishers

Other leading-edge business books
from Berrett-Koehler Publishers

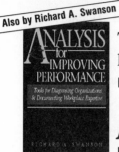
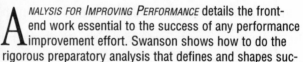

Structured On-the-Job Training

Unleashing Employee Expertise in the Workplace

Ronald Jacobs and Michael Jones

JACOBS AND JONES describe an approach to on-the-job training that combines the structure of off-site training with the inherent efficiency of training conducted in the actual job setting. They show how structured OJT helps employees bridge the gap between learning job information and actually using that information on the job. *Structured On-the-Job Training* provides step-by-step guidelines for designing and delivering effective training in the actual job setting.

Hardcover, 220 pages, 1/95 • ISBN 1-881052-20-6 CIP
Item no. 52206-279 $29.95

Moving from Training to Performance

A Practical Guidebook

Dana Gaines Robinson and James C. Robinson

MOVING FROM TRAINING TO PERFORMANCE shows how today's performance improvement departments can take a more active role in helping organizations meet their service and financial goals. It offers practical, action-oriented techniques from some of the most highly respected contributors in the field—Geoff Bellman, Geary Rummler, Paul Elliott, Jim Fuller, Harold Stolovitch, Erica Keeps and other experts-paired with real-life case studies of organizations such as Johnson & Johnson, Andersen Consulting, Prudential HealthCare System, Steelcase, PNC Bank, and others that have achieved exceptional results by successfully making the transition to performance at each level of alignment.

Paperback, 300 pages, 7/98 • ISBN 1-57675-039-6 CIP
Item no. 50396-279 $29.95

Performance Consulting

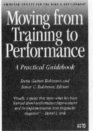

Moving Beyond Training

Dana Gaines Robinson and James C. Robinson

PERFORMANCE CONSULTING provides a conceptual framework and many how-to's for moving from the role of a traditional trainer to that of a performance consultant. Dozens of useful tools, illustrative exercises, and a case study that threads through the book show how the techniques described are applied in an organizational setting.

Paperback, 320 pages, 1/96 • ISBN 1-881052-84-2 CIP
Item no. 52842-279 $24.95

Hardcover, 4/95 • ISBN 1-881052-30-3 CIP • **Item no. 52303-279 $34.95**

Available at your favorite bookstore, or call (800) 929-2929

On-The-Level
Performance Communication That Works
New Edition

Patricia McLagan and Peter Krembs

DESIGNED TO HELP managers and employees plan and execute more effective and less fearful communication, *On The Level* provides tips, action steps, and practical tools to help everyone in and around the workplace communicate "on-the-level."

Paperback, 140 pages, 8/95 • ISBN 1-881052-76-1 CIP
Item no. 52761-279 $19.95

The Future of Staff Groups

Daring to Distribute Power and Capacity

Joel P. Henning

THE FUTURE OF STAFF GROUPS teaches staff groups—groups within organizations that perform internal functions such as human resources, finance, legal, quality, information systems, and others—how to shed old patterns and roles and speak directly to the concerns of their clients, their managers, and the groups themselves.

Hardcover, 190 pages, 10/97 • ISBN 1-57675-025-6 CIP
Item no. 50256-279 $29.95

Preferred Futuring
Envision the Future You Want and Unleash the Energy to Get There

Larry Lippitt

LARRY LIPPITT details a proven process for mobilizing a whole human system to envision the future they want, then develop strategies to get there. *Preferred Futuring provides the practical tools needed to develop clear action plans that* link vision to action and spirit, with bottom-line results.

Paperback, 240 pages, 10/98 • ISBN 1-57675-041-8 CIP
Item no. 50418-279 $24.95

Available at your favorite bookstore, or call (800) 929-2929